Road to Recovery

ROAD TO RECOVERY

Following your
Motor Vehicle Accident

Lawrence Matrick MD

GRANVILLE ISLAND
PUBLISHING

Library and Archives Canada Cataloguing in Publication

Matrick, Lawrence, 1933–, author
     Road to recovery : following your motor vehicle accident / Dr. Lawrence Matrick, MD.

Includes index.
ISBN 978-1-926991-42-9 (pbk.)

1. Traffic accident victims—British Columbia—Handbooks, manuals, etc.
2. Traffic accident victims—Legal status, laws, etc.—British Columbia—Handbooks, manuals, etc. 3. Personal injuries—British Columbia—Handbooks, manuals, etc. 4. Automobile insurance claims—British Columbia—Handbooks, manuals, etc. I. Title.

HE5614.5.C2M37 2014   363.12'5409711   C2014-907556-1

The characters in this book are fictitious. Any resemblance to actual persons, living or dead, is purely coincidental.

Editors: Brenton Leith and Sheilagh Simpson
Proofreader: Kyle Hawke
Book designer: Omar Gallegos
Indexer: Bookmark: Editing & Indexing

Granville Island Publishing Ltd.
212 – 1656 Duranleau St.
Vancouver, BC Canada V6H 3S4

604-688-0320 / 1-877-688-0320
info@granvilleislandpublishing.com
www.granvilleislandpublishing.com

First published in 2015
Printed in Canada on recycled paper

To my wife Jean and also to our children: Marilyn, Diana and Michael for their love, encouragement and support while writing this book and also for travelling with me on this journey

Contents

Introduction

Having a motor vehicle accident and an injury is bad enough, but sadly that's not the end of it. Then you find yourself buried by the volume of forms, treatments, appointments with consultants, meetings with lawyers . . . and the list goes on and on. I have seen many people who have been involved in a motor vehicle accident, being overwhelmed by the added stress of the medical-legal process. If you are one of these people, reading this book will help you to understand the medical-legal relationship as you prepare your injury claim.

I am a qualified physician and psychiatrist, in practice for many years. I have written hundreds of independent medical evaluations, or IMEs. I have been qualified by the courts as an expert witness dealing with people who have been involved in motor vehicle accidents, or MVAs. Almost every patient I've seen in this capacity is nervous or frightened before and during the consultation.

This book discusses many important questions that people like you have asked me over the years.

Questions like:
- How do I deal with the insurance company?
- Do I need a lawyer?
- What type of doctors and other therapists will I need to see and what type of therapy will I need?
- And, most importantly, will I get better?

Many of you are confused and fearful about what might happen next. This book aims to help you by explaining what your lawyer and all those consultants actually do. Use it as a reference when you have an appointment with a specific consultant so that you may know what to expect and how to be prepared.

This book also has many suggestions and strategies to help you deal with other aspects of your life that have been affected by your injury, like anxiety, sleep disorders and relationships. I hope, by guiding you through this very lengthy medical-legal process, to ease your mind and renew your hope and optimism for the future.

It is not my intention to give legal counsel or to tell you how to proceed. I can only offer suggestions, explanations and various recommendations as to the kind of consultations that you might encounter and the purpose of these consultations. Your lawyer, insurance adviser and your family doctor will be your best counsel, guide and advocate.

This book can also help you deal with the added medical-legal stress by giving you guidance so you can be prepared for the unknown. It will tell you something about the legal process, the types of medical disorders you may encounter and some of the more common therapies and treatments that you will be offered.

Be prepared! Be aware! Knowledge is power!

I wish you the best in your recovery from your injuries. I hope that you are able to obtain good medical care and legal advice, and that you receive acceptable compensation for all the pain and suffering, as well as the many losses and challenges.

CHAPTER 1

Your Legal Obligations and Insurance Coverage

Melody

Melody, a 25-year-old immigrant from Korea, knew her tips would be the best she'd ever seen after the New Year's Eve party at the sushi restaurant. Kim, another Korean she worked with, had gone ahead to try to find them a table at the bar across the street.

Melody worked quickly to close up the restaurant. She cleaned her tables, mopped the kitchen floor and then counted her tips. Over two hundred dollars — it had been a good night.

She pulled the heavy black wool scarf over her head to keep her ears warm and buttoned her black overcoat before she walked out into the cold, damp night. She locked the front door and stepped onto the sidewalk full of rowdy revellers, hooting and hollering, clanking cowbells and blowing cardboard horns.

Excited about her date with Kim, she rushed to the crosswalk and, as the walk signal flashed, she stepped off the curb. With all the noise, her ears covered and all in black on that dark night, neither she nor the drunk driver swerving around the corner saw the other. The car, loaded with young people, bowled her over backwards, smashing her right shoulder against a newspaper box. A pedestrian shouted at the car, but got only the finger from the driver, who sped off. He helped Melody up and asked if he should call an ambulance.

"No, no. I'll be all right," she said, massaging her shoulder. She wasn't going to go to the hospital and miss her night out with Kim.

Melody was pleased to see that a police officer down the road had flagged down the drunk driver for going through a red light and hitting her at the crosswalk.

Your legal obligations and insurance coverage

If you are involved in a motor vehicle accident, you have a number of legal obligations to the police and to your insurance carrier. Depending on the extent of damages, most provinces have minor differences regarding these notifications. However, *all* accidents involving injuries or death, hit-and-run, suspected impaired driving, an out-of-province vehicle or where a vehicle must be towed from the scene must be reported to the police *immediately*. Even in the case of a minor fender-bender where there are no injuries, failing to call the police in order to settle privately can lead to major complications. For example, the other party could later deny the amount of damages or even deny being the driver or try to sue you for personal injuries of people who weren't in the car. Without witnesses, photos or a police report, you could end up having to pay all costs or be in litigation for a long time, at great expense.

Do you need car insurance?

Wherever you live in Canada, having car insurance is very important. All vehicles operating on public roadways *must* be insured. Insurance protects you against another party's claims if you are responsible for an accident resulting in death, injury or damage to the other vehicle or property damage. It can help you in case you are unable to work and can provide for your family if you are permanently injured or killed. If the other party in the accident doesn't have insurance or is underinsured, your policy can help to make up for any shortfall in his or her insurance coverage. Finally, your policy can pay for the cost of repairing damages to your vehicle or for its replacement, depending on the type of insurance you carry.

It is important to understand that there are a variety of different options when it comes to insurance, both in terms of the amount of coverage and the type of coverage. It is always best to discuss your insurance needs with a qualified and trusted insurance broker.

Some points to keep in mind:

- Underinsured Motorist Protection (UMP) is meant to protect you in the event that the at-fault motorist has insufficient insurance to cover all your losses. It is relatively inexpensive, and you are well-advised to obtain as much UMP insurance as you can.

- Collision coverage will cover the cost of repairs to your vehicle if you are at fault in an accident. If you don't have collision coverage and you are at fault, the cost of repairs to your vehicle will not be covered.

- The most important thing is that you are truthful when you apply for your insurance. Your insurance will be void if you are untruthful as to things like who the principal operator is or whether or not you will be driving the vehicle to work.

In Canada, insurance is purchased for a term of one year or less and is required on all vehicles being operated on public roadways. Generally, your insurance will be valid in Canada and in the United States. If travelling and renting a vehicle, you should check with your insurance company to see if your coverage extends to it. Be aware when driving in the U.S. that third-party coverage can be very low or non-existent. This means that if you are involved in a collision with a U.S. motorist, there is a very good chance that they will not have sufficient insurance coverage to compensate you for all the losses you suffer, and that you will have to rely on your UMP policy for full compensation. Most policies are not valid in Mexico, and you should purchase additional insurance upon arrival at the Mexican border.

Again, it is important to purchase the appropriate amount and type of insurance when you acquire a vehicle. Policies can vary depending on the type of car you purchase — you should talk to your insurance agent and get his or her advice about the coverage you need. If you are uncertain about what sort of coverage you should have or how to proceed, ask a relative, friend or neighbour to go with you when you speak with an insurance agent. You must fully understand what your responsibilities are and what you are signing.

Legal obligations to the police and insurance providers

In British Columbia, the Motor Vehicle Act requires you to remain at the scene of an accident, to render assistance, to exchange information with the other driver and to report the accident to the police if damages exceed $1,000. Remember that a slight scratch or a dent from a minor fender-bender can be very expensive to repair and can easily cost over $1,000. If you leave the scene of an accident without reporting it to the police or if you do not exchange information with the other parties, you might be in violation of the Motor Vehicle Act and your insurance provider can hold you in breach of your contract of insurance, resulting in your insurance being void. You should never walk or drive away from the scene of an accident without ensuring that you have fulfilled your legal obligations. If you do, your insurance provider might assume that you had something to hide, like impairment, which could put your coverage in jeopardy and cost you a lot of money.

In most provinces, if the damage is minor and there are no injuries, you don't have to call the police. In Ontario, for example, if there are no injuries and damage appears to be less than $1,000, the police might not attend, but you must report it to the Collision

Reporting Centre within 24 hours. In Alberta, you must call the police if the total damage is over $2,000. Alternatively, in some U.S. states, you are required to call the police if damages are as low as $500, while other states require police notification only if the damages exceed $5,000. If you are driving in the U.S., you should check with the police, your insurance provider, the rental car company or a lawyer to ensure that you understand your responsibilities and can protect your rights.

If you hit a dog or cat, you can call the police to get information on how to proceed. You must call the police if you hit a larger animal such as a cow or horse. In either case, you should let your insurer look after all future dealings with the owners of the animal in order to protect yourself from future legal or other complications. If you are injured in an accident involving an animal, it is advisable to seek legal advice, as there are occasions when you will be entitled to compensation for injuries or losses.

Again, while the police might not attend a minor fender-bender, you should call them after an accident and follow the procedures described below.

What to do if you are in an accident

It is important to read the instructions in the pamphlet supplied by your insurance provider when you purchase a policy. Many such pamphlets will have a section listing the details you should record in the event of an accident. These instructions can also be found online, at a police station and in libraries or other public buildings. Be sure to read these instructions carefully and be informed of all your responsibilities.

The following is a partial list of what to do after an accident:
- Stay calm and make sure that both you and any others involved in the accident are out of harm's way, especially on a busy roadway.
- Turn on your hazard lights and call the police or 911.

- If anyone is injured, administer first aid and wait for emergency crews. Do not move anyone who has been injured unless failure to do so puts them at further risk.
- Exchange insurance details with all other drivers involved. Record their names, addresses, phone numbers, licence information and their insurance company names and policy numbers. Make sure to get not only the driver's information but also the vehicle owner's, if these are different people.
- Talk to any witnesses and passengers and get their names and phone numbers.
- Take photos of the accident scene, the vehicles and the people involved.
- Do not leave the scene of the accident until all information has been exchanged and either the police have arrived, if they have been called, or a decision has been made to not call the police.
- Do not by any means accept any form of payment from the other driver. Your refusal to take money at the scene of the accident does not mean that the other person has lost the right to pay the damages directly. He can negotiate this directly with his insurance company, but then you have the protection of having the insurance company involved.
- Do not sign any documents other than a police report.

Call your insurance company as soon as possible after an accident and do not repair your vehicle before dealing with your insurance company. When you contact the insurance company, make sure that all information provided is accurate. Notes are kept by all the people and agencies you deal with, from the police to the initial 'Dial-a-Claim' phone call, so if anything you have said later turns out to be untruthful or wrong, it could have a significant impact on how your claim is dealt with.

If you have the slightest doubt about your legal obligations, call the police!

Private vs. government insurance in Canada

Across Canada, there are over one hundred private insurance companies providing coverage. In British Columbia, Saskatchewan, Manitoba and Quebec, government-owned insurers provide the compulsory component of auto insurance, with private insurers competing with them to offer additional optional coverage. All the other provinces and territories have only private insurance carriers.

What will insurance cover?

Insurance coverage is very detailed and specific, but you must talk with your agent to understand exactly what coverage you require and to ensure that you have the insurance you need. Briefly, you should understand if your insurance company might cover the cost of medical treatments and therapies that might not be covered under your provincial or state medical plan. Provincial medical coverage in Ontario, for example, has certain limits, so any additional amounts should be covered by your policy. Other coverage might include disability income if you are unable to work, which will provide regular payments depending on both your past income and the degree of disability. Other policies can also cover funeral expenses and provide a death benefit to your next of kin. You must talk with your adjuster or agent to understand exactly what benefits are available to you.

If you are involved in an accident while driving to or from work, the Worker's Compensation Act might come into effect. In that situation, your insurance company might refer you to the Worker's Compensation Act and the appropriate government agencies for assistance. There are specific time limits that must be complied with in dealing with the Worker's Compensation Board, so do not delay in reporting the injury to them. If the at-fault motorist is not a worker within the course of their employment at the time of the accident, your right to sue for fair and full compensation for your injuries and losses is preserved, despite the fact that you are a worker at the time of the accident. Be sure to seek legal advice if this is your situation, as an experienced lawyer will be able to help you determine the best way to proceed.

Caution

If you are in a collision while your licence is suspended for any reason, driving illegally will nullify your insurance coverage. That noted, your insurance will most likely pay on claims against you, but will then seek reimbursement from you directly for all claims paid out on your policy. Insurance companies have a number of different mechanisms available to them to force you to pay, including preventing you from getting further insurance or being able to renew your driver's licence. If you are in this situation, speak to an experienced lawyer as there are a number of ways that a resolution to the insurance company's claim could be negotiated without you paying the full amount that was paid out on your behalf. In such cases, damage to your vehicle will likely *not* be covered by your policy.

No-fault insurance

No-fault insurance means that if you are injured or your car is damaged, you deal with your own insurance company regardless of who is at fault. In provinces with no-fault insurance, insurance companies assign the percentage of fault for each of the drivers involved in the accident. In Ontario, for example, if you skid on ice and rear-end another car, the fault determination rules state that "a car that rear-ends another car is at fault," regardless of the road conditions. The insurance company will apply your percentage of fault and then determine the amount of deductible, if any, that you have to pay. If you are fully or partially at fault for an accident, the insurance company will likely increase your insurance premiums on your next renewal date. Quebec, Manitoba, Alberta and British Columbia also have no-fault insurance.

In many provinces, including British Columbia, Alberta, Saskatchewan and some Maritime provinces, in addition to no-fault insurance, there is an option to sue to recover fully on the damages that you have suffered as a result of the accident if you are not at fault. The availability of this option varies throughout Canada. If you are injured in an accident that is not your fault, seek advice from an experienced personal injury lawyer, who will be able to advise you of your rights to compensation.

Liability coverage

If you are being sued because of an accident, your third-party liability coverage will be accessed to pay any potential damages, up to the limit of the insurance policy you purchased. While each province has its own policies, in British Columbia the basic coverage limit is $200,000 for damages for which you are responsible. You can purchase additional coverage to increase this third-party liability amount. Some agents recommend coverage levels from three to five million dollars. The compensation necessary to make whole injured parties in a motor vehicle accident often exceeds $200,000, as your third-party liability coverage has to cover everyone injured in the accident and the vehicle damage, regardless of the number of people injured. You will be personally responsible for anything over and above the amount of your third-party liability coverage. For this reason, you should always purchase as much third-party liability coverage as you are able to afford.

What are non-pecuniary damages and awards?

'Non-pecuniary damages' is a legal term for an award or damage(s) as a result of pain and suffering and loss of amenities in life after your accident. This means that you have lost the ability to enjoy those aspects of your lifestyle that you were active in prior to the accident. For example, you might no longer be able to walk as well as you used to, enjoy your hobbies, participate in sports or experience intimacy in your relationships. It is also meant to cover such things as the discomfort you experience as a result of your injury, the inconvenience of the injury and the myriad other effects that an injury has on you that are not directly linked to a calculable monetary loss.

What are pecuniary losses and awards?

Damages awarded to a not-at-fault party following a motor vehicle accident are meant to return you to the position you would have been in if you had not been injured in the motor vehicle accident. An award of non-pecuniary damages might not be sufficient to do this and you might also be entitled to pecuniary damages. Pecuniary damages are monetary damages that can be calculated, and can include out-of-pocket expenses such as treatment costs, wage loss and damages for loss of future income-earning capacity. A comprehensive future-care plan might also require payment of a number of items in the future to ensure that you are fully compensated. Each situation is unique. An experienced personal injury lawyer can give you advice based on your specific situation about the pecuniary losses you will be entitled to.

Suing for damages

Depending on which province you live in, you may or may not be able to sue the other driver, and the differences between the provinces are substantial. As each province has different policies, you must again confer with your agent and the insurance company to fully understand your legal rights. If you are a passenger in a vehicle driven by a family member or a friend found to have been responsible, or even partly at fault, you might have to sue that person in order to receive insurance benefits. For obvious reasons, this can be problematic for everyone involved and could cause serious disharmony for years to come. Remember, you are suing not to punish that individual but rather to make sure that you are made whole for all the losses you have suffered due to the accident. The friend or relative will not be personally responsible for the damages, rather their third-party liability coverage will be accessed to provide you with the payment. Regardless of whether or not you sue, the at-fault motorist will face consequences with their insurance company, such as increased premiums.

If you decide to hire a lawyer, don't be alarmed when the insurance company also hires a lawyer to represent the motorist you are suing. One of the benefits your third-party liability coverage provides is legal assistance in case you are sued. The insurance company lawyer will have access to your medical records and could require you to see additional doctors, medical consultants or therapists to better understand and assess your injuries.

Private insurance providers

Private insurance is the norm outside of British Columbia, Saskatchewan, Manitoba and Quebec. Even in these provinces, private insurance can be purchased to cover additional items such as liability, damage to your vehicle or wage losses. Most such policies state that claims must be made within a definite period of time. This can vary from 15, 30 or even 90 days after an accident. You must be aware of and fulfill the terms of your insurance company's specific filing requirements or they might not be obligated to honour your claim. Third-party insurance might also assist you with your accident if it occurred out of your home province or in the U.S. If you are confused or have language barriers, you might want to talk with your insurance agent, a lawyer, a relative or friend to ensure that your coverage is sufficient and that you meet all of the requirements of the policy.

Keeping good records

It is important to keep a log of all expenses and a day-to-day journal of your injuries, complaints and visits to doctors and therapists. You should also keep all medical care bills and receipts, as well as other costs regarding medicines and prescriptions. Keep an account of what was discussed at all medical, legal or insurance agent meetings. Keep copies of all letters and e-mails and document telephone conversations, including a careful record of all communications. These documents and records will be very helpful to you, your legal team and your insurance agent as your case proceeds.

Depending on where you live in Canada, there are certain time limits for filing your claim. In British Columbia, for example, insurance claims must be submitted within 30 days of an accident and any subsequent lawsuits must be filed within two years. Private insurance policies also state that claims must be made within a definite period of time which, again, can be 15, 30 or even 90 days after an accident. You must be aware of and fulfill the terms of your insurance company's specific filing requirements — or they might not be obligated to honour your claim.

The Insurance Corporation of British Columbia (ICBC)

As the following information applies primarily to claims made in British Columbia, be aware that this information might differ in the particular province in which you are making a vehicle accident claim. Once again, this is only a summary. You should seek advice from your insurance company or from a lawyer for information pertinent to your situation.

The Insurance Corporation of British Columbia (ICBC) is the primary auto insurance company in the province of British Columbia and provides third-party liability as well as accident benefits and basic Uninsured Motorist Protection (UMP).

Contacting ICBC

You should contact ICBC as soon as possible after an accident. You can do this by phoning them, by visiting a claim centre or by contacting them online. In each case, an ICBC representative will ask for information you gathered at the time of the accident. If the police attended or if the accident was later reported to them, you should include the police case file number. All information provided to the ICBC representative will be recorded and passed on to the adjuster who will be dealing with and evaluating your claim. Generally, the ICBC representative will also schedule a meeting with an adjuster, to discuss the details of your claim. If English is difficult for you, ask to have an interpreter or family member assist you. Once you have contacted your insurance provider, you can also bring in a lawyer to act on your behalf.

Evaluating your claim

An ICBC insurance adjuster will meet with you and ask you to describe, in detail:
- what happened
- what your injuries are and how they are affecting you
- what treatment(s) you have had
- where you were working at the time of the accident
- if you were able to return to work
- what your income was

If you have an injury claim, you will have to fill out accident benefit claim form CL-22, describing the accident and the injuries you sustained. This is a legal form that can be used as evidence in a lawsuit or in court, so you must be very specific and clear in what you say or write. Furthermore, you will be asked to provide an expense list if you needed medical treatments or equipment, a description of how your lifestyle has been affected by the accident and any police report describing who was at fault. You will also be asked if you were wearing a seat belt and if your headrest was properly adjusted. If you were on a motorcycle or bicycle, you will be asked if you were wearing a helmet. If you have any difficulties with the English language, you should bring an interpreter to the meeting. This can be a friend or a relative. If you are still doubtful about anything, you should again consider calling a lawyer to act on your behalf.

Your claims adjuster might also ask you to sign certain forms that permit them to access records from your hospital, doctor or other therapists you have visited. Be aware of what you are signing — ask your adjuster to explain the document and what it might be used for, as it will give the insurer access to all of your medical records, even those long before the accident. You can ask the adjuster to limit the release to only information after the accident.

Following the meeting, and upon review of the police reports and medical reports, the adjuster will assess your claim to determine what benefits you qualify to receive.

The personal injury claim and no-fault benefits

Everyone injured or killed in a motor vehicle accident in Canada has coverage. Everyone driving in Canada has some type of coverage for medical, rehabilitation, death and wage-loss benefits. However, each province has different amounts available and it is very important to know what amount is available from your specific provincial insurance, private insurance or a combination of these. Depending on the insurance in your particular province, there might be a maximum level of benefits available, but you will also be covered to some extent by your provincial medical services plan for medical evaluations and treatments.

These benefits are available regardless of who is at fault and are called 'no-fault benefits' or, in British Columbia, 'Part 7 benefits'. This means that you can seek compensation if you have been injured, regardless of whether the accident is your fault or the fault of another motorist. You will not be entitled to anything other than the available no-fault benefits if the accident was solely your fault. If you are a pedestrian or cyclist who has been injured by a vehicle found at least partially at fault for the accident, then you will have an insurance claim either through your provincial government insurance corporation or the motorist's private insurer. In this kind of situation, your injuries and any disability plus medical expenses might be covered, but you must check this with your provider or with your lawyer.

No-fault coverage can include payment of medical expenses, rehabilitation and other therapies, wage loss, replacement of homemaking services, funeral expenses and possibly death benefits to next of kin. Depending on the policy and the province, some therapies and consultations might not be covered, so check with your insurance adjuster or agent before starting treatments. You will likely also have to submit an Accident Benefits Application form to receive benefits — your adjuster will explain this form to you. Adjusters may be arbitrary in the way they decide whether they will cover treatment. If you have access to damages beyond the no-fault benefits, any expenses that are reasonably incurred will be recoverable. You should rely on your medical practitioner's advice in terms of choosing whether to pursue treatments, rather than the adjuster's decision about whether the cost of the treatment will be covered.

In hit-and-run claims, ICBC or your provider in other provinces is required to pay awards on injuries, damage to a vehicle or death benefits, even if the at-fault motorist is unknown, as long as certain conditions are met. You have to have made reasonable efforts to ascertain the identity of the unknown motorist or you will not be entitled to any compensation. What is reasonable depends on the circumstances, but it is always advisable to do everything you can to identify the other motorist. In a situation like this, you should try to find witnesses to the accident. You could advertise for witnesses in a local newspaper, notify the police and post notices in the area to see if anyone saw the accident. You must make a claim and take your vehicle in to the insurance company for inspection.

Underinsured motorist protection claims or Underinsured Motorist Protection (UMP)

Unfortunately, some drivers, especially in the U.S., have limited or no insurance coverage. If you are in an accident where the at-fault vehicle has limited or no insurance, insurance carriers offer Underinsured Motorist Protection, or UMP. There might be limitations on collectable benefits, so check with your insurance provider, especially if you are travelling to the U.S.

With UMP coverage, your insurance provider could also ask you to recover the money by suing that person, in which case you might need a lawyer to recover the monies. Under certain circumstances, depending where the accident occurred, ICBC or your insurance provider elsewhere will make payments under the UMP claim. Everyone covered by ICBC in British Columbia has UMP coverage up to $1,000,000, but you can also purchase optional additional coverage through ICBC. All provinces across Canada have similar coverage as part of the basic mandatory policy.

If you have a problem with your provider

If you have a difference of opinion with your insurance provider anywhere in Canada, you might be able to settle the problem by contacting the manager of the claims department, who might be able to offer other assistance or advice. A commissioner or other authority will help you with your problem. If you are still unhappy, you should talk to a lawyer about your options.

Remember that it is very important to keep notes about all phone calls, meetings, e-mails, texts or written letters that you have with your lawyer, the insurance company, friends, doctors, therapists or other witnesses. Keep a log or calendar of what you are doing and what was said to anyone, including what advice you received following the accident. This should include meetings with your physician, any reports received, therapies and notes from employers as to the loss of wages due to injuries.

Melody

Melody did not have to sue the driver of the car as he was found fully at fault. She was happy to have her case settled by working directly with her adjuster at ICBC. After a few months of physiotherapy combined with massage treatments, she recovered from her shoulder injury and returned to work on a graduated basis and with the support of others. She also continued to see Kim who went into business for himself. On full recovery, Kim made her the manager of his very successful Korean restaurant. They now live in an apartment, above the restaurant, with their twin baby girls.

CHAPTER 2

Independent Medical Evaluations (IMEs)

Michael

"What a great morning for a bike ride!" Michael said to Jason, his young son. Michael maneuvered his new Santa Ana Grand LX bicycle along the narrow street.

As Jason attempted to pass him, Michael turned to tell his son to slow down — that's when the accident happened. Neither he nor his son saw the car door swing open. Michael hit the door full-force and careened up and over it. He felt searing pain in his left elbow as he tried to get up from the pavement. He felt faint, he couldn't move his left leg and his back was in spasm. He tried to crawl to the curb on all fours, but fainted from the severe pain in his hip. That was the last memory Michael had until he heard the distant wail of an ambulance.

That was two years ago. Last week Michael opened a letter from the lawyer he had hired soon after the accident. The letter said that he had an appointment to see a psychiatrist the following week. In the previous twelve months, he had seen a neurologist to assess the ulnar nerve damage in his left elbow and an orthopedic surgeon who recommended hip surgery. On the advice of his lawyer, he also saw a counselor, which he paid for himself. The counselor told Michael that he seemed depressed and should consider seeing a psychiatrist.

The physiotherapist he saw for his back spasms wrote a letter to Michael's lawyer stating that Michael suffered a stress disorder. Michael remembered that his own doctor and the chiropractor had said he was tense and anxious.

"I suspect you're suffering from post-traumatic stress, Michael," the physiotherapist told him as she performed a deep neck massage for the whiplash he had suffered. The whiplash hadn't been diagnosed until almost two years after the accident, but it was finally receding, thanks to the physiotherapist.

Susan, Michael's wife, wasn't pleased when she saw the lawyer's letter. "A psychiatrist?," she said. "What for? You're nervous, not crazy."

Michael was troubled too — he paced back and forth all evening. He couldn't sleep because of nightmares, then he finally moved to the couch to avoid disturbing his wife.

Michael had been on extended medical leave for two years. The long-term disability payments barely paid the mortgage, so his wife had returned to her evening shift job at a restaurant. Michael borrowed money from his in-laws and increased a loan from the bank. As money became scarce, his son Jason, a talented goalie, had to drop out of hockey school. His daughter Emma had to stop ballet classes.

Michael, anxious, depressed and still in pain, spent his time seeing medical consultants, fretting in waiting rooms of physiotherapists and massage therapists and seeing private counselors he couldn't afford.

The future looked grim.

Independent Medical Evaluations (IMEs)

As a direct result of your accident any or all the following may apply to you. You have lost your health, been unable to work and are falling into debt. You are in constant pain and are unable to walk or exercise like you used to. You shun your friends and your family does not understand how much pain you are in. Your children think you are weird because you are ignoring them and behaving differently. You just lie around. Your intimate relationship with your partner is suffering because of pain and depression. You're afraid to take medications like sleeping pills, tranquillizers or antidepressants in case you become addicted.

As if that isn't enough stress, now you have to worry about the uncertainty of your medical-legal situation. Perhaps two or perhaps three years have passed since the accident, and you may still need to see more medical consultants who will write reports on your condition. You've already been that route, but you know you have to do more.

These meetings are called Independent Medical Evaluations (IMEs) or examinations. Your lawyer, insurance provider and disability carrier will want you to see qualified medical consultants who can provide expert opinions regarding your injuries, whether they are physical or psychological.

These meetings can be tough and scary.

Attending an Independent Medical Evaluation

Serious accidents may involve obtaining a settlement, either from the at-fault party or from an insurance provider. Such a settlement depends on proof, which can be determined by many factors, including medical evidence. While your own physician's records and reports are important, independent medical evaluations, conducted by various medical consultants might be required to provide medical documentation to assist in a final legal judgment.

After the first or second year following your motor vehicle accident, you will likely have seen a number of consultants or therapists. By the third or fourth year, you may have seen every specialist and therapist outlined in the following chapters. In fact, you might see the same consultant more than once, and then others in the same field, in order to get a final diagnosis and a prognosis on treatment and recovery.

Reasons for IMEs:

- Your insurance or disability providers could require an IME to assess the extent of your injuries or determine the short- to long- range prognosis.
- Your lawyer, or those of the party you are taking legal action against, may want to have an independent specialist examine you to get an opinion on your injuries and disabilities.

An IME can be ordered by your own lawyer or by the lawyer for the other side, if your physical or mental injuries are at issue. You could be required to see more than one examiner to determine the extent of your physical or psychological injuries, and you might not have a choice of whom you are going to see.

The consultant who is doing an independent medical examination is, by rule, not allowed to discuss the conclusion or the therapy with the patient. It is an objective independent assessment and, therefore, recommendations, diagnosis and treatment may not be available to you at that time. This can be awkward for you, but the examiner will likely explain this.

Seeing a consultant or expert usually arises after you've hired a lawyer.

CHAPTER 3

Hiring a Lawyer

Michael

Right after his accident, Michael considered hiring a lawyer. He suffered soft-tissue injuries, which may last a long time. Soft-tissue injuries are those involving supporting, non-bony parts of the body such as muscles, ligaments and tendons. Such parts may tear, sprain or strain causing severe soreness. He also fractured his left elbow, bruised his left hip and received a serious whiplash when his head bounced off the pavement. An MRI indicated that he might need more surgery because a nerve in his left elbow was out of place. Since Michael was left-handed, he couldn't work. He also had a bad limp from the steel pins in his hip.

His family was now dependent on bank loans and financial help from his in-laws since his long-term disability policy expired. His neighbour and friend Marilyn said, "If you decide to seek legal advice, Mike, you could probably get an opinion from a lawyer free of charge on the first meeting."

Michael was worried because the defendant's insurance provider wrote him a letter stating that their consultant concluded that with elbow surgery, he might not have a permanent injury. Michael heard that in order for a lawyer to take his case, he might have the option of paying a retainer up front or going on a contingency-fee basis, in which the lawyer's fee is taken once the case is settled.

Before he met with the lawyer, Michael reviewed the lawyer's website to see if it was professionally presented. He read the information available regarding the lawyer's experience.

Michael made sure that he had all the information required regarding the accident. He had his own notes about the accident including exactly what happened, the individuals and witnesses involved, and the time and location. He could also provide the lawyer with all the documents that he had been given after seeing his doctor and therapists.

Michael's lawyer explained that he would work on the case on a contingency fee that would be paid once the case was settled.

Hiring a lawyer

After an accident, those who wish to make a claim may go to their insurance carrier and meet with an adjuster. The adjuster assesses the validity of the insurance claim on behalf of the insurance company and has the ability to authorize payments or repairs. It is very important to talk to a lawyer before filing insurance forms. The lawyer can review your case and help you complete any forms so that they are thorough, accurate and to your benefit.

Before meeting with a lawyer, you might consider researching his or her website to ensure that they have the professional experience required and that they present themselves professionally.

Most lawyers will provide an initial consultation free of charge. If retained, a lawyer will require that payment up front or on a contingency-fee basis. A *contingency fee* is what your lawyer charges once the case is settled. The amount, which can be up to 33 and 1/3 percent (or higher with court approval), is deducted from the final settlement.

Preparing to meet with an attorney

You should make sure that you have all the information in regards to the accident before meeting a lawyer. This includes descriptions of exactly what happened, statements from the individuals involved and any witnesses, the time and location of the accident and notes about the accident including weather conditions. The lawyer will also require copies of all the documents provided by doctors, therapists and any other service providers employed as a direct result of the accident.

After preparing as completely as possible, then you make an appointment to meet the attorney.

General questions that you might ask the lawyer:
- Who will pay for the specialists if I need treatment?
- Can I see the proposed fee agreement?
- Can I pay on an hourly basis?
- If I paid on an hourly basis, do I pay each time I visit or can I pay after the settlement?
- Will you charge me for phone conversations?
- If we agree to a contingency-fee basis, what percent would you take off the final settlement?
- What services are covered by the retainer or contingency fee?
- What additional expenses can I expect to be billed for?
- Will other lawyers in your firm also be working on my file?

All applicable fees should be detailed in the standard agreement between you and your lawyer.

Your lawyer should be able to identify whether or not you may be entitled to financial compensation for loss of future income-earning capacity, cost of future care and other possible incurred fees and future medical expenses. Some out-of-pocket expenses may also be covered, which might include certain other costs such as transportation to therapists, medical or mobility equipment and house cleaning or gardening services.

You might also ask the lawyer if you are found to be either partially or entirely at fault, whether any financial settlement would be reduced by the percentage you are deemed to be at fault. That is, if found to be at fault, you may receive a partial or no financial settlement and could be held liable for any costs incurred.

The lawyer's role

Your lawyer will be able to inform you of your rights and provide you with advice so you can be fairly compensated. With her specialized knowledge about the value of claims, she will gather and organize the information to argue your case, will negotiate on your behalf and, if necessary, take your case to court. Remember that while representing your interests, a lawyer's loyalty is *not only to you alone, but also to the court.*

Keep in mind that any legal claims may have time limits in different jurisdictions. If you miss one, you may not get compensation for your injuries. *You should see a lawyer as soon as possible and be aware of your responsibilities.*

It is very unlikely that you would have to go to court and have a judge make a decision about your case. This depends on liability and the type of damage claim.

Negotiation means that your lawyer will talk to the insurance carrier and negotiate a settlement for you. *Mediation* is when opposing parties agree to meet one another with a professional mediator called in to help disputing parties reach an agreement. If your case cannot be settled through negotiation or mediation, then you must talk to your lawyer about other options. Many issues can affect your claim. Evidence has to be gathered from the police, any witnesses and from numerous medical personnel.

Some issues might include:
- Whether you have been totally or partially responsible for the accident
- The nature and extent of your physical injuries

- The nature and extent of your emotional injuries
- How much and what type of treatment you may need
- Whether or not you have been left with a total or partial disability
- Whether or not you may be able to return to the same job
- What pre-existing injuries you may have had and your overall health condition prior to the accident

This is only a partial list and your lawyer will explain more fully the various issues that could potentially affect your claim.

Most of the compensation you may be entitled to could come from the defendant's or at-fault driver's insurer, as the process is dealing with third-party coverage. In some jurisdictions, the insurance provider may provide insurance coverage for *both* drivers, but you must talk with your lawyer about this.

Remember, a lawyer will work to protect your interests — you might not have to negotiate directly with an insurance provider.

CHAPTER 4

Mental and Psychological Assessments and Independent Medical Evaluation (IME)

Michael

On his lawyer's recommendation, Michael agreed to see a psychiatrist for an independent medical evaluation. The lawyer asked the psychiatrist to determine what psychiatric problems Michael exhibited, whether they were caused by the motor vehicle accident and what treatments might be required.

However, like many people, Michael was confused about the differences between psychiatrists, psychologists and counselors.

Mental and psychological assessments and independent medical evaluation

Psychiatrists, psychologists and counselors are therapists who deliver psychological treatment, but each has different educational requirements and is regulated to provide only certain kinds of therapy.

Before seeing a therapist, you will need to have all the information about the motor vehicle accident and injuries you have developed prior to your appointment, with copies of the notes and reports from all doctors and hospitals you have visited. Expect to discuss what life was like for you both before and after the accident. Again, if there is a language barrier, ensure that a translator is included in the consultation process.

A *counselor* has generally received special training in a specific area such as school counseling, religious counseling, grief counseling or genetic counseling. Some may have a college diploma or university degree or be an accredited nurse or social worker. Many have years of experience and expertise. Be aware that some people who call themselves counselors have limited training and experience. Ask your physician or whoever referred you for a character reference about the counselor, and ask the counselor about his qualifications and experience during your first visit.

A *psychologist* is a well-qualified therapist who can help you work through emotional problems. Psychologists are university graduates who have earned either a Bachelor of Arts (BA) or a Bachelor of Science (BSc), then, possibly, a master's degree such as a Master of Arts (MA) or a doctorate (PhD). While PhDs are called 'doctor', they are not medical doctors and do not prescribe medications.

Extra medical coverage through your workplace may pay for some therapy sessions. Since these services are not covered under provincial medical plans, you may have to pay privately.

A *psychiatrist* is a fully-licenced medical doctor, who has earned a medical degree (MD) and then specialized in the field of psychiatry. In Canada, psychiatrists must receive their degree from the Royal College of Physicians and Surgeons of Canada (RCPSC) to be qualified to work as practicing psychiatrists.

Many psychiatrists have a private practice, while others work in community mental health clinics, teach at universities or work in hospitals. You can expect the psychiatrist to provide an office for the examination, to make the proper psychiatric evaluation and to have the report completed promptly and available to the lawyer. Your psychiatrists must comply with certain legal requirements and certify that they are not an advocate for any party.

Psychiatrists who see you for an independent medical evaluation have a responsibility as an external expert to remain unbiased, independent and objective.

The psychiatrist cannot give you an opinion at the time of the visit, but will mail an extensive report to the lawyer or the insurance provider who requested the IME. These reports usually include a statement whether any psychiatric disorders they may have discovered are the result of the motor vehicle accident. Finally, the psychiatrist might suggest a treatment program and recommendations for referrals to the appropriate consultants.

Since psychiatrists are medical doctors, their services are covered by provincial health plans. However, to receive this coverage, you must be referred by another physician, usually your family doctor. The exception to this would be a private consultation or IME requested by a lawyer or an insurance provider. The lawyer may refer you to a psychiatrist of their choice for an IME, and the lawyer will pay the psychiatrist directly. The fee, as a disbursement or expense, must then be paid as part of your final settlement. In the case of a referral from an insurance company, union or other agency that wants an opinion, the referring agency should pay the bill, but confirm this beforehand.

Michael

Michael's psychiatric report stated that he was suffering from a major depressive disorder with severe anxiety, panic attacks and social phobia. He was also suffering from post-traumatic stress disorder and, possibly, a mild traumatic brain injury, which would require further evaluation.

The report also stated that the psychiatric disorders all seemed to be a direct result of the motor vehicle accident. Finally, the psychiatrist suggested a treatment program and made recommendations for referrals to other consultants for further opinions or therapy, including a referral to a psychologist.

After the consultation and therapy with the psychologist, Michael felt more hopeful and optimistic about his recovery. He looked forward to meeting with his lawyer again to prepare for the discovery meeting, which is explained in the next chapter.

CHAPTER 5

The Examination for Discovery

In an examination for discovery, you, your lawyer and the lawyer for the other side will meet in the court reporter's office or in a boardroom. Your lawyer will meet with you prior to discovery to prepare you and acquaint you with the process. A court reporter will record, transcribe or document everything that is said under oath. The other side's lawyer will ask you questions. It is your responsibility to answer these questions truthfully.

During this meeting, both sides will likely produce medical documents. These meetings can be lengthy, but your lawyer will be there to support you. Both sides may take breaks as necessary.

What happens in discovery?

The examination for discovery process allows the lawyers from both sides to review medical documents that may be presented and any other available evidence. The opposing lawyers might want to question you about your medical health before the accident and if you had any pre-existing medical conditions. Your hospital records, family physician records and independent medical evaluations may be available during this meeting. It is important for you to be polite, calm and truthful during these meetings.

During discovery, both sides will evaluate you as a witness, review documents and document the process. Each side is required to commit to the evidence provided, which can be challenged later at trial if there are any changes. At discovery both parties can *ask for documents and information about your case*, but your lawyer will be there to support and protect your interests before, during and after the discovery process.

Answer all the questions you are asked, stay focused, take your time, and be calm, polite and truthful.

Listen carefully! Pay attention!

Listen to each question carefully. Do not answer a question you don't understand, and do not start answering a question before the lawyer is finished asking it. If you are unsure of the answer, or if you cannot remember, then say "I don't know" or ask for questions to be restated or clarified. Pay attention, and don't go off the point, deviate or ramble.

Be polite to all the participants and remember that *everything* is on the record. During discovery, your lawyer will make sure you are being treated fairly and will object if he deems any question improper. In order for the other side to understand to what extent you are disabled, you may be asked questions about your personal life, including, in some cases, details about your intimate relationship(s) and sexual life.

Discovery can lead to a settlement offer from the insurance company. However, if an offer falls short of expectations, your lawyer may recommend going into mediation.

Michael

A few days after the discovery meeting, Michael saw his lawyer again. His lawyer reviewed the results of the discovery procedure with him and told him that a reasonable offer had been made.

They discussed the offer being presented and assessed the benefits of proceeding further.

Michael considered his options. After almost three years, he had finished with all of the medical consultations and all the therapies, including surgery to his elbow. He had followed through with all of the recommended treatments and was well on the road to recovery. If he chose to pursue things, the next step could be mediation, arbitration or, finally, going to trial. Those options could take much more time. He considered the amount of stress, not only for him, but also for his family.

Michael and his family were exhausted by all the medical consultations, therapies and the strain of the whole process. Since he was close to being fully recovered, he made the decision to accept the offer and conclude his legal action. If he had decided not to accept the offer, his next step may well have been mediation, which will be described in the next chapter.

CHAPTER 6

Mediation

Sital

After studying all day, Sital, an accounting student at the end of her course, needed a walk to clear her head of numbers and tables. She was pleased to have just landed her first job with the government, subject to passing her final exams next week. Bundled up in her warm woolen coat, the young woman waved goodbye to her mother, and stepped out into the wet snow that had been falling all day.

Sital snapped open her umbrella and smiled as she thought about plans to help her mother make curry-spiced samosas tomorrow at their temple. She picked up her pace, avoiding the slush and dirty snow on the sidewalks, and drew nearer to the busy boulevard.

The light had just changed, and when she saw the walk symbol telling her it was safe, she began to cross the street. It was then that Sital heard the skidding of tires on the slush-covered street. But it was too late to react. An SUV making a right turn slid right into her.

Sital was knocked over into the grimy sludge and almost pinned down by the front of the SUV. Dazed, confused and scared, she looked up to see the car's front bumper above her left shoulder. The right front wheel was almost touching her left hip.

The older man driving the SUV jumped out of his vehicle, shouting obscenities. Traffic stopped and a young woman ran across the street to help Sital out from under the vehicle and onto her knees. Then she called 911 on her mobile phone. The woman helped her to move onto the sidewalk.

Sital brushed the greasy black slush from her coat. "I'm okay," she assured the woman. "This heavy coat saved my fall."

The driver just stood and glowered. "I couldn't see you in that black coat and dark hat!" he shouted, not even asking her if she was hurt.

'Why is he blaming me?' Sital thought as she slowly pulled herself to her feet.

"I had the walk sign," she said to him as she dabbed the blood from a scrape on her forehead. As the man neared her, she could smell alcohol on his breath.

She and the driver exchanged names and phone numbers.

"I don't need an ambulance, thank you," she said to the two policemen who arrived. Sital didn't want to go to the emergency room. Not now. She still had to finish her exams next week and get ready to start a new job.

She noticed that the officer questioning the driver was administering a Breathalyzer test, and then led him, handcuffed, to one of the police cars.

Sital limped home, rubbing her left shoulder and dabbing the blood from her forehead. At home, her mother made her tea and gave her a pain reliever. Then she went to bed.

The next day, she went to the emergency department with crippling neck and back pain, a sore hip and a left arm she couldn't lift. The doctor diagnosed whiplash and soft-tissue injuries to her chest, and ordered an X-ray of her left shoulder and left hip. He gave her a prescription for pain relief and suggested she see a massage therapist and a physiotherapist.

Sital deferred her exams for a week and confirmed that she could start the new job a few weeks later. After three months of therapy, however, she was still in pain and on medication. She *struggled to stay focused, to keep her new job. After another six months, her doctor suggested she speak to a lawyer.*

It took some time for her lawyer to arrange an appointment with the orthopedic surgeon who would do an independent medical evaluation, and then she had to wait several more months to see him. The surgeon determined that there were no broken bones and that she would heal over time. After several more months on pain medications, dealing with pain at work and attending massage treatments, physiotherapy and chiropractic treatments, Sital's lawyer suggested the possibility of mediation as a way to settle her case quickly.

A few days after the mediation session with her lawyer and the insurance company, Sital met again with her lawyer. The insurance settlement offer was presented in a package that they carefully reviewed together. Her lawyer had already countered the offer, requesting that it also cover certain additional medical therapies. The insurance company lawyer agreed and Sital signed the papers. She was hopeful that between the continuing massage therapy and physiotherapy treatments, she would have a full recovery.

Sital was grateful to her lawyer, and even more grateful to end her more than two years of stress, fear and frustration. She continued to recover and her ability to focus and her concentration improved, greatly improving her employment as an accountant. At the end of that year, her employer recognized her performance improvements.

Her mother organized a party at the temple to celebrate her hard work and good fortune. Sital's mother, sisters and aunts were up all night making samosas. Over two hundred family members, friends and neighbours attended the celebration.

Mediation

Mediation is a process whereby a trained mediator (a third-party intermediary) helps you, your lawyer and the insurance provider work toward a settlement. Mediators are often attorneys or retired judges. The mediator may not advise you what to do, so any decisions belong to you, with your lawyer's guidance. Mediators cannot force either party to accept anything. Instead, they attempt to make it easier to come to a settlement by making recommendations to promote a fair compromise. In a typical car accident case, you might have an agreement within a day.

Your lawyer will meet with you and prepare you for the mediation many days before the process is due to begin. She will coach you about how to tell your side of the story effectively and explain what to expect from the other side. During mediation, your lawyer will present your case to the other side. This includes each side presenting a *mediation brief*, which is a detailed summary stating their position. This document is given to both parties and to the mediator before mediation takes place.

The mediation process

All parties and the mediator meet together in either lawyer's office or in a private room. The mediator explains that he or she is a 'neutral' party and gives a general introductory statement as to what the case is about. The mediator might summarize the main problems or any disagreement between the parties.

Both parties will share their positions with one another and with the mediator. You may be disappointed in the other lawyer's position, but remember that these statements are early and pre-liminary. Everyone may also discuss settlement without worrying about the case going to court; statements made in mediation by either side are confidential and are inadmissible in court.

There could be extensive discussion by the group as a whole. Your lawyer might advise you to answer specific questions to clear up some aspects. Remember that you are free to consult in private with your lawyer before saying anything. The mediator will be present throughout, but may separate the parties from time to time, speaking privately with each side and carrying new proposals back and forth. During such a 'break-out' session or separation, the mediator may help each side see the other's perspective and also tell you and your lawyer about possible weaknesses in your claim.

At any time during the mediation, either side can leave the room to talk about an offer. The other side may start with an offer, but this can change as negotiations develop. You may also negotiate directly, but do so only on your lawyer's advice.

The mediator can talk to both sides and present offers and counter-offers until an agreement is reached. It will be up to you and your lawyer to decide how to respond to any offers or counter-offers made by the insurance company representatives.

You will probably have to decide whether you want to accept a settlement offer or go to court, which would take more time and add further stress. Remember, if you decide not to settle through mediation, there are other steps available to you. You should discuss these with your lawyer. If you and your lawyer do agree to a settlement, you will have to sign a settlement document.

Mediation costs money and your lawyer may charge you for time spent in preparation as well as the time during the mediation process. If your lawyer is on a contingency basis, however, then you will have no extra charges. There may be other charges to cover the additional costs of the process. It's advisable not to go into mediation unless you are really interested in reaching an agreement.

Your lawyer can present a proposal, with your approval, covering all of the damages the two of you feel that you are entitled to receive. This might include lost wages and payment of past, present and future medical expenses related to your injuries. Future recommended treatments and costs would be determined from the IME reports from your various consultants.

CHAPTER 7

Arbitration

Chen-chi

Chen-chi was celebrating her 50th birthday by going for a hike up a local mountain with her three adult children, who were visiting her from Chicago, Toronto and San Francisco. They would all be going to Hong Kong soon to see her 90-year-old auntie.

The snow was crisp and the sun warm. Chen-chi carried a red flag so the snowmobilers, also on the hill, could easily see her group.

The trail up the mountain was easy for Chen-chi. She was in good shape — and was grateful to her yoga instructor for that. She laughed at the three city slickers, huffing and puffing, trying to catch up to their mother.

As she made a sharp turn in the path, she heard her son shouting something behind her. She also heard the whine of the snowmobile motors coming up on her right. To make way for the snowmobiles and a rowdy group, shouting and tossing beer tins into the trees, she moved off the trail and onto a roadway used by other vehicles.

The snowmobilers whizzed by her, churning up a blizzard of white snow and temporarily blinding her. Bewildered by the chaos, she continued to cross the road. She didn't see the car with two hunters coming at her.

Chen-chi couldn't remember much after that. She did remember the cold ice against her cheek. Her face was covered in snow and her right hip was painful and her right leg was useless. It was very cold and she shivered violently. Chen-chi's children huddled around her, knowing not to move her.

"Are you alright, lady?" the frightened young truck driver said. "I tried to swerve, but the crazy snowmobilers were in my way." He called 911 on his cell phone, as Chen-chi's children huddled around her, knowing not to move her.

She lay there in the deep snow, drifting in and out of consciousness and shivering as the sun dipped below the horizon. Her children had covered her in jackets. They waited for the mountain safety patrol and the stretcher.

Chen-chi had surgery to her right hip. She was well cared-for and her children stayed with her. For the next six months, she followed through with her doctor's referrals for physiotherapy. She was then diagnosed with chronic pain syndrome.

Her lawyer told her that the driver had received a minimal fine for reckless driving. The problem was that he was not insured, he was visiting from Europe and he could not be found.

Three years after the accident, Chen-chi's orthopedic surgeon told her that she would need to wear a neck brace because of the arthritis in her back and her right knee would soon need surgery.

Chen-chi was in despair. She was on permanent disability leave from her job as a licenced practical nurse at the local hospital and needed chronic pain management and antidepressants. She continued physiotherapy and massage therapy.

The driver of the car still could not be found.

Chen-chi's lawyer explained that in her case arbitration might be an agreeable option in light of the underinsured motorist protection limits. He explained that an arbitrator might set a financial limit, but that there may be limits due to third-party insurance and foreign accident limitations.

"This way, you may get an agreeable settlement, and it can be settled quickly," her lawyer said.

In the fourth year after her accident and after her day in discovery, on her lawyer's advice, Chen-chi opted for arbitration.

Arbitration

Arbitration is an agreement to settle a dispute through an arbitrator, who acts as a referee and whose decision is binding upon all parties. You and your lawyer may have some decision in choosing the arbitrator. The arbitrator, who may be a retired lawyer or judge, sits in the contested hearing between you, your lawyer and the defence. Then, acting as a judge, he has the power to render a legally-binding decision. In arbitration, each side can call witnesses, including any or all of the medical consultants you have seen.

The arbitrator will hear all the arguments for and against you, review the evidence and then make a financial award decision. It is less formal than a court trial and can be less time-consuming and less expensive. This might not be the case, however, if the process becomes lengthy.

Advantages
- You can choose the arbitrator with your lawyer's advice, but if you go to court, you cannot choose the judge or jury.
- Arbitration is often faster and cheaper than going to court.
- Arbitration is private, whereas a court case is public.

Disadvantages
- Arbitration can be lengthy and complicated because of the many medical or other witnesses called.
- The other side may pressure you for many more IMEs, which could be costly, but this might also happen with a trial.
- Arbitration is binding, and the arbiter's decision is final. If you disagree with the decision, you have no future recourse.

- You may also have to pay for the arbitrator, which could be costly relative to other options.

Consult with your lawyer as to whether he believes arbitration is the way for you to go.

Chen-chi

Chen-chi received a settlement through arbitration, which was very acceptable to her. Six months later, after a knee replacement and rehabilitative physiotherapy, she was able to walk again using a cane.

After another six months of therapy, she returned to her job on a graduated return-to-work basis in an administrative position, at a desk.

Five years after her accident, Chen-chi took her family and the three adult children to Hong Kong to pay tribute to their auntie at her gravesite. The cemetery was up a small hill overlooking the city, which Chen-chi was able to climb slowly with the help of her cane.

CHAPTER 8

Going to Court

Joanna

"Yer not to see that pot-head Josh again, ya heard me?" Joanna's mother called down from the upstairs landing.

"Don't worry, Ma. He got his driver's licence back last week," Joanna answered, excited to have just turned nineteen and be going to a bar. She dabbed her lips the crimson red that Josh liked and pinched her breasts up over her bra.

"Yeah, well, don't be late. Yer father goes to bed at eight."

"Yeah, yeah, Ma. I'll be up early to phone that guy at the mall for the job."

Joanna knew that Josh would take her to park in the woods for an hour, smoke some killer chronic and then hit the bars near the US border.

When she heard the car horn, Joanna ran down the wooden steps and waved at Josh. He was waiting impatiently at the curbside, leaning on the horn.

Josh passed her a joint as she climbed into his '62 Ford Galaxie and she could smell the stale beer on his breath.

"You shouldn't be drinking," Joanna chided as she smoothed down her miniskirt. "Remember what happened last time. You know — that fender-bender," She didn't fasten her seat belt. It always left bruises on her right breast and Josh didn't like that.

Josh gunned the motor, leaving black tread on the pavement. The neighbours would be complaining to Ma again, Joanna mused.

He sped well over the limit, down the country road that was clear and straight for miles, but still damp from last night's heavy rainfall.

Joanna gripped the rust-weathered dashboard in front of her. "Hey man, slow down!" she said. "We have an hour before we have to meet everyone." Then she added, "Did you get those new brake pads you said you needed?"

Josh ignored her and leaned over to run his right hand up her skirt. He drained the beer can with his other hand and floored the gas pedal even harder. Then he turned onto a gravel road.

"New pads? Yeah, yeah," he sneered. "Next week. When I get paid."

Those were the last words Joanna ever heard from Josh. Suddenly, the Ford careened over a fallen tree branch and a large pothole, then spun out of control and struck a cedar tree with such force that the tree fell on the driver's side of the car.

The impact threw Joanna forward into the dashboard and windshield.

She passed out.

The excruciating pain in her legs woke her up. The metal dashboard and the still-steaming engine were in her lap and the windshield was shattered all over the inside of the car. She couldn't move her right arm, which was pinned by mangled metal.

"Josh, Josh, are you all right?" she moaned, wiping glass and gelled blood from her eyes. She couldn't see out of her right eye, but looked towards the driver's seat. Josh's eyes were wide open, staring into nothing. He was dead, she was sure of that, pinned to the seat by the tree limb when it came through the windshield.

Joanna couldn't catch her breath — her heart was pumping against her chest. Still pinned under the burning heat of the motor and in excruciating pain, she tried to push open the door. *Fighting the urge to pass out again, she reached into her purse for her cell phone and called 911. She was sure that this was the end as smoke billowed up from the front end of the car. She lapsed in and out of consciousness.*

A siren sounded in the distance. The rescue crews moved around the car, pulling the old Ford apart with the Jaws of Life. At one point Joanna told someone that it was strange that her left leg was pointing away from her, at right angles, and her right hand was numb. Her last memory before she drifted off again was the emergency room nurse asking her something.

Two days later her left leg was amputated just above the knee. Later she realized that her right elbow was frozen stiff from multiple fractures and several pins and screws, and she was blind in her right eye. Then the doctor told her she had suffered a severe brain injury.

Two years later Joanna was able to walk on flat surfaces with an artificial left leg, but her right hand was a permanent claw. The pins and screws had been removed from her right arm and elbow, but she was not able to bend it. In the third year after the accident, she couldn't remember anything about it. Her concentration was bad, she couldn't focus on reading and her memory was poor. She was irritable and bickering with everyone all the time.

The rehabilitation therapist told her she had a chronic brain disorder from her head injury and would probably be on permanent disability for years to come.

Five years after the accident and after seeing multiple consultants for many therapeutic sessions, her lawyer suggested that it was time to consider settling her case. All the medical consultants reported that she was indefinitely disabled, which meant, he said, for a very long time, if not for the rest of her life.

Her lawyer suggested that she might get a better financial settlement by going to court.

She simply nodded in agreement.

Going to court

If you decide to go to court, then you are called the plaintiff: the person who starts the legal action. The person or party being sued is called the defendant: the person against whom a legal action is brought. You might decide to go to court if you have suffered a crippling or disabling injury needing life-long therapy. Or you might want your day in court because you are angry about being severely injured and want to see the defendant punished. This last reason can be very expensive. Court expenses might be taken out of your final monetary reward. Also, your final settlement may be reduced because you have to pay for all medical consultants and other costs and disbursements.

Litigation generally takes a long time, usually years, and is a lot of work for everyone involved. Settling outside of court can save time, energy and money for everyone. You, on the advice of your lawyer, may decide to settle before your case goes to court.

Legal fees for trials may cost more because it generally takes longer to prepare for a trial, especially if you are paying the lawyer on an hourly basis. On a contingency-fee basis, there could be a staggered progression of charges with one kind of percentage-based agreement if settled out of court and a different kind if it goes to trial. A trial may also be more stressful for you and your family, with long delays due to postponement. And you may be on local TV, radio or the newspapers, since court is public.

Any financial reward received may depend on the seriousness of your injury or other factors such as fault, whether impaired driving is involved, wages or employment losses or other expenses incurred. Severe injuries, such as broken bones, severed limbs, or brain damage, may receive a higher settlement. You might also receive a higher settlement if you are unable to return to work or will require rehabilitation and future retraining.

The court process

You and your lawyer, or the other side, may opt to have your case heard by either a judge or a judge and jury. Your doctor, and any other medical consultants or character witnesses, may be called upon to testify. The lawyers for each side can question these witnesses at length. The judge is able to ask questions of witnesses or either side's legal representatives. In a jury trial, once all the evidence has been presented, the judge may instruct the jurors on the laws that apply to the case. The jury will deliberate, and then present its conclusions to the court. In Canada, if the jury rules in your favour, the judge decides on any financial compensation.

Third-party litigation funding

Third-party litigation funding can help finance your court case, but you should consult with your lawyer about this decision. In Canada and the USA, there are companies that offer litigation financial services. This is an offer of financial backing if you need money to pay for your legal costs. These plaintiff's loans might vary in percentage of the amount of your final reward. In some cases, you will not have to pay until you receive a settlement. If the settlement you receive is not enough to repay the loan, you will have to find money elsewhere to pay the balance.

Representing yourself in court

You are not required to have a lawyer represent you, even in court, so you can represent yourself. However, there are many rules of procedure and evidence that must be followed, and you may find yourself in over your head if you try to represent yourself. The opposing side *will* have lawyers that know the rules, and you run the serious risk of being unable to prove your case. If you have a case worth bringing to court, I strongly recommend hiring a lawyer to represent you. The possible exception is in small claims cases, which usually involve only small debts.

Joanna

On her lawyer's advice, Joanna decided to ask for a jury trial. The idea here was that the jury should see her — see the damage done to her face and the severity of her injuries, with her artificial leg and limited movement in her arm. All her consultants gave evidence that she had severe disabilities and would need home-help and years of therapy, and that she was totally unemployable in her current state.

The court ruled in Joanna's favour and she received enough money that, when invested, provided her with an adequate monthly allowance to pay for her basic expenses for the rest of her life.

CHAPTER 9

What to Do
at the Scene of an Accident

Joel

"It's okay, Franco," Sammy shouted as he winked at the blonde sitting at the bar. "Give Joel another. Just one for the road. Joel's a good buddy."

Joel waved at his good friend in gratitude and downed his sixth lager, with a brandy chaser. "Yeah, jes' one mo for da road," Joel slurred, as he wiped the spittle from his chin.

"No, man. No more," Franco yelled back. "You're way over the limit. You get in an accident and I lose my job."

Sammy defended his friend. "He's walking his dog, Franco, not driving! Come on! You know it's not the same." Franco looked out the doorway at a brawny bulldog tied to the lamppost outside the bar.

Another drink would make no difference to Joel by this point, Franco figured, and he handed him another beer.

Joel finally waved farewell and staggered out the door to the dog. 'My ex got the house, but you're all mine, aren't ya, Winston?' he thought, as he untied the leash from the post and looped it around his wrist.

Winston pulled Joel along their regular route across the railroad tracks toward their home on the other side of the highway.

Joel swayed unsteadily and held on to the leash as Winston led him across the ditch beside the road. Joel was too drunk to think about traffic — he didn't even look to see the sleek black Porsche speeding towards them. It hit Joel head-on at ninety kilometres per hour.

Joel went flying onto the hood and slid down along the windshield, landing on the roadway beside the Porsche. Winston was hit and tossed aside.

The leash was still looped around Joel's wrist when the car stopped and the driver and his passenger jumped from the Porsche. They found Joel unconscious on the pavement with blood oozing from both ears. Winston was lying on his side whining softly. Three cars stopped, but the female passenger still in the Porsche waved them off.

Joel's head rolled unnaturally from side to side as the passenger pulled him up into a sitting position and yelled at him to wake up. It was then that the driver of the Porsche and his passenger heard the noise of another car smashing into the Porsche, and then two other rear-enders followed in quick succession.

The result was chaos. People shouting, the highway blocked, cars honking — another accident just waiting to happen.

The ambulance and fire trucks were on the scene quickly and immediately secured the scene. Winston lay on his side whimpering. The paramedics worked on Joel, who still hadn't regained consciousness. They rolled Joel onto a stretcher and took him to the hospital. He was declared dead on arrival.

A vet put Winston down the next day.

What to do at the scene of an accident

Each year, people are injured or killed while attempting to assist others at the scene of an accident. They unwittingly put themselves or others at risk while trying to help. Only those with specific training who know how to assist the professional emergency personnel when they arrive should do this. Depending on the jurisdiction, untrained people who try to assist may face legal ramifications.

In basic first aid, you are taught how to keep the injured party or parties alive and stable until a professional rescuer takes over. I strongly recommend that you enroll in a first-aid course with cardiopulmonary resuscitation (CPR) and Automated External Defibrillator (AED) components. Recognized courses are generally available through your local community centre, fire or police departments, the Red Cross, St. John Ambulance, the YMCA or the YWCA.

Keeping in mind that this is a general guide only, let's look at some basic first-aid measures.

First aid

First, you must assess the accident scene to ensure that no one else, including yourself, can be injured by oncoming traffic or other threats. You will be of no use to the injured person if you rush in and get injured or killed. Think about the dangers the accident scene presents to you and to others. That is, is it safe for you to approach the scene? Is fuel leaking? Is there a safe working area? Is there an electrical or fire danger? Are there any other dangers to you or others?

While you survey the environment, call 911 or ask someone on the scene to do it and to confirm with you when it's done. Whoever calls, 911 may ask that person to stay on the line until rescue crews arrive.

If possible, send someone to surrounding buildings for first-aid and AED kits. All public buildings and businesses are required to have a first-aid kit and many also have AEDs, which, when turned on, provide automated step-by-step instructions.

Once the scene is secure, look at the victims. Those having the most life-threatening injuries take priority. Unconscious or unresponsive casualties should receive immediate attention.

Don't panic. Remember the ABC technique.

The ABC technique

The aim of the ABC technique is to keep an unconscious person alive until emergency crews arrive. If you deal with the three ABC essentials, you may save a life.

Airway — is the person's airway clear?
Breathing — is the person able to breathe?
Circulation — is there a pulse or any blood loss?

Speak to the unconscious person, identifying yourself in a gentle and firm voice. Explain what you are doing as you check them over. This has the added effect of helping you keep yourself calm and focused while assisting.

A. Airway!
Keep the injured person as still as possible in case the spine or neck has been injured. You may need to gently lift his chin to ensure he is not choking on his own tongue. Unless there is imminent danger to staying where he is, do not move him in any way!

B. Breathing!
Place your face just above the casualty's mouth, look down along the person's chest for movement of the chest, feel and listen for breathing. If she is not breathing, begin CPR. This is a procedure that you can learn from professionals during a first-aid course. If you don't know how to do this, call 911, and the operator will describe how to do it.

C. Circulation!
If the person is not responding, check for a pulse to see if their heart is beating. Use the carotid artery in the neck to get a pulse. Finding the pulse can be difficult. If you are having problems,

check the pulse on both sides of the neck or on the left inner wrist. If you are unable to find a pulse, begin CPR until an AED arrives or emergency crews take over. After checking the pulse and breathing, check for any signs of bleeding. Try to locate any wounds, putting pressure on the injury to stop the bleeding.

You now have the basic information to complete an ABC assessment. You know to check the casualty's airway, breath and pulse.

If casualties are conscious, do not move them, as there may be spinal cord or other internal injuries. Identify yourself and tell them not to move while you survey the other casualties. If you find someone you believe to be most in need of attention, ask if you can help that person. Find out his or her name, age, and ask if he or she has any pre-existing medical conditions or are experiencing any pain or difficulties. Keep the person calm and ask what happened. Try to keep the victim warm and do not let the person have anything to eat or drink until after the ambulance personnel arrive and approve it. When the ambulance arrives, give the professionals all the information you have gathered regarding the casualties — and then stay out of the way. Do not leave the scene until cleared to do so by the emergency personnel.

Joel

Remember what happened to Joel and his poor dog Winston! Like drunk driving, drunk walking is very dangerous. Drunk walking is not only a danger to the intoxicated person but potentially to others as well.

CHAPTER 10

Ambulance Crews and the Emergency Room Physicians

Zahrah

Zahrah passed a deer-crossing sign, a warning to drivers to exercise caution. Like many others on that northern highway, she tended to ignore such signs — she rarely saw any animals, and the weather was clear that morning, except for a slight fog.

Zahrah was a midwife, the only one to serve two small mining communities and the aboriginal reserve in the remote northern part of the province. A patient's husband had called her in a panic. His young wife, he said, was in labour. It was the couple's first child. Zahrah was rushing to get to her side.

Zahrah slowed down as she came into a tight curve at the bottom of a hill. It was then that she saw the young deer on the side of the highway. Suddenly, it sprinted across the road. Zahrah was momentarily distracted by the deer's grace.

She never saw the large stag that darted out of the woods to her right. She struck the stag head-on. The huge animal bounced onto the hood of her car and smashed through the windshield. Her Jeep swerved off the road and rolled into the ditch.

The seat belt snapped open and Zahrah was thrown out the driver's door by the force of the impact. She lay in the shallow ditch, in shock, barely conscious. Her right leg was smashed and her back was in spasm.

The Jeep's engine was belching acrid smoke. Zahrah could smell gas. She crawled away, pulling her right leg behind her. She felt around in her jacket pocket for her mobile and called 911. Just before she lost consciousness, she saw the buck shake off the blow and lope across the roadway.

Zoning in and out of consciousness, Zahrah thought she heard an approaching siren coming from the reservation on the other side of the small lake. Later, as the ambulance crew attended to her leg, she saw a helicopter land on the highway — her transport to a hospital in the Lower Mainland.

Zahrah was seriously injured, freezing cold and in shock, but she remembered to tell the paramedics about her patient who was having a baby. One of them assured her that they'd take care of it.

Zahrah received emergency care for injuries to her hip, legs and back. Following an ER consultation with an orthopedic surgeon, she underwent hip and leg surgery.

Ambulance crews and emergency room physicians

After a serious accident, your life may depend on the quick work of the highly-trained ambulance personnel who respond. In Canada, these people are called paramedics, and are usually dispatched by a 911 operator. On arrival at an accident scene, the paramedics assess your medical condition and ask you about any pre-existing conditions such as heart problems or diabetes.

As discussed in the last chapter, the first thing that 911 responders do is take a quick survey of the accident scene and make the area safe for ambulances, fire crews or police — and for other drivers approaching without knowledge of the accident. The side of the road is a very dangerous place and emergency personnel will often block off the scene with their vehicles.

If you are injured, the paramedics will probably do a preliminary survey, including the ABC's: airway management, breathing and bleeding control. Then they will move on, recording other injuries and stabilizing you for transfer to a hospital. If necessary, crews will remove you from your vehicle as safely as possible. You might be immobilized (secured so that you cannot move) on a board or stretcher to prevent or limit possible neck or spinal cord injuries.

On the way to the hospital, the paramedics will provide life-support procedures. For example, if you have breathing problems, they may provide oxygen via a plastic mask placed over your nose and mouth. If you need fluids or medication, these will be given to you via an intravenous line, a tube delivering the fluids directly into your veins. Or you may need intubation whereby a hard plastic tube may be placed in your mouth and throat to help you breathe.

Even if you seem to have no broken bones or internal injuries, you are still advised to go to the closest emergency room and it is always best to go by ambulance. You should not drive yourself — you may faint, collapse or get dizzy and be in another car accident. Nor it is advisable to have someone else drive you. The driver may panic and start speeding or driving dangerously to get to the hospital, and may cause another accident.

It may not be to your advantage to refuse the ambulance. If the case later goes to court, the opposing side or the judge could say that you were perfectly fine to drive and that your vehicle was in good working condition.

Even if the accident seems to be minor, you should always go to the emergency room to have a thorough check-up. This might also help show that you have a valid and legitimate claim, as required by your lawyer. If you avoid treatment, the judge or jury may conclude that your injury may not have been that serious, and you may not get a favourable settlement.

Do not exaggerate or lie when you are in the emergency room. Insurance adjusters and lawyers will have copies of what ER doctors write in their report, including any statements you might make.

If you are unable to return to work after the accident, you should ask for a note from a doctor to this effect. Some emergency room doctors will give you such a note, others will tell you to get it from your family physician. Your insurance provider or your disability insurance policy usually pays for the days you are unable to work.

The ER physician will probably be the first to provide a thorough medical assessment. After that, while you are still in the hospital, other specialists such as neurologists, neurosurgeons and neuropsychologists may be brought in to consult. These consultation referrals can also come *after your discharge from hospital and by your family doctor.*

I strongly recommend that, after an accident, you go to the ER by ambulance and have a thorough checkup.

Zahrah

Zahrah did not go home immediately after her discharge from hospital. She remained with friends in the Lower Mainland for several weeks so that she could receive physiotherapy and massage treatments.

Back in her own community, Zahrah remained on disability while she recovered. She returned to work as a midwife two years after her accident.

Although Zahrah had been unable to deliver the baby because of the accident, the paramedics arrived on time and assisted in the delivery of a nine-pound baby girl.

The grateful mother called the baby Sarah.

CHAPTER 11

Family Physicians

Roy

"Okay, Jackson, hurry up," Roy said, pulling on his rollerblades. "Let's get going! The weather's clearing."

"The rain may have stopped, but the road's still slippery," Jackson replied, looking nervously at the busy traffic. "I'm kinda worried. I fell pretty good last time, man." The sun slowly burned off the haze hanging over the city.

"It's going to be a scorcher. Let's go!" Roy shouted.

Jackson, with a tender knee from a recent fall, had bought the best pads he could find. Out on the street, he braced himself against the telephone pole and hesitantly pushed off.

Roy was already half a block ahead as Jackson approached the intersection. The light was still green, so Jackson sped up, trying to catch the light and keep up to Roy.

As Roy rounded the corner, a bicycle courier with a large pack sped through the red light, against the traffic. Two cars slowed down and honked their horns as the courier speedily snaked his way through a group of pedestrians.

He came right at Roy.

Roy couldn't stop, swerve or get out of the way. He was sideswiped by the aggressive courier and went head over heels into the path of a delivery van.

The delivery van driver slammed on the brakes, trying to avoid Roy, but he hit him and threw him to the ground. Roy fell heavily, his head striking the pavement. He rolled onto his side, doubled over in pain. A pedestrian ran to his side and tried to help him off the street.

"Don't touch him, mister!" the driver yelled, as he drove away. "He might have broken bones. I'm already on the phone with 911."

Roy was aware only of the severe pain in his right hip, numbness in his right hand and a searing frontal headache. He vomited his breakfast all over his skates as he tried to sit up.

Jackson saw the courier look back, but he didn't stop.

"You better go see your doctor, young man," an elderly lady wheezed at him. "You better go and do that, you hear? I broke my hip two years ago, so I know what I say. You hear me?" She stood over him, continuing to talk.

Other people offered to help, but Roy waved them off, embarrassed. He didn't want trouble. "Oh, I'll be fine. Thanks, anyway," Roy said, brushing the grime from his legs and massaging his right hand.

He also waved the ambulance and the police away, refusing any more help or assistance.

"It's all right. I'm okay," he said, wincing in pain and shaking his head as the paramedics tried to persuade him to take the waiting ambulance.

As the ambulance drove away, Jackson took his friend by the arm and flagged down a passing taxi. He was younger than Roy, but wiser. The cabbie took them to a medical clinic a few blocks away.

Family physicians

Visit your family doctor as soon as possible after you've been released from the hospital after an accident. If you don't have a family doctor, go to your preferred walk-in clinic and arrange to see the same doctor for all future appointments or go to the emergency department of the nearest hospital. Tell your doctor everything about the accident. This includes all the details of your injuries — just start from the top of your head and gradually move down to your feet. Describe your pain in detail, using words like radiating pain (pain that does not stay in one place), needle-like, sharp, dull, ongoing, numb, shooting, tingling or burning.

Some very important reasons to see your doctor after an accident:
- to diagnose your injuries and determine the adequate treatment
- to discover if you are well enough to go work
- to get the correct forms for disability from work so you can get paid and get referrals for treatment
- to have everything on record for your insurance carrier and/or your lawyer

Ask your doctor for a note for your employer. You may also ask him for a copy of all his notes, treatments and referrals — be aware there might be a processing fee. Keep a file at home for your lawyer and insurance agency — in it, put all police reports, ambulance reports or any other information that comes your way.

Follow your doctor's recommendations. This is referred to as compliance, or obedience to treatment. It is really important to remember that all future doctors, lawyers or the courts can ask you if you followed the doctor's instructions.

Your doctor could prescribe X-rays or other examinations, order medication, physiotherapy, chiropractic care, massage therapy or refer you to different specialists. Doctors' notes are also for their own legal protection. If you do not follow your doctor's orders, that non-compliance could be noted in your file and may be used against you in your legal case. Your insurance provider's lawyers could argue that you didn't try to get better. This could mean the difference between receiving proper compensation for your injuries, or not.

Roy

Roy made a terrible mistake by waving off the paramedics and by not going to the hospital in the ambulance.

Fortunately for Roy, his friend Jackson made sure he received medical attention shortly after the accident. On the clinic's recommendation that he follow up with his own doctor right away, Roy dropped the ball, waiting almost a week.

In the end, though, Roy did listen to his doctor. He kept good notes of his injuries, pains and his slow recovery. He also consulted a lawyer, giving him all the notes, documents and reports that he had on file. Those notes also helped his doctor prepare the medical reports for his lawyer and other medical consultants, and helped Roy make an insurance claim through his company health insurance policy, which covered medication and additional rehabilitation expenses like physiotherapy.

Tell your doctor about any pre-existing medical conditions, that is, illnesses that you had before the accident. Some illnesses could add time to your recovery or prevent injuries from healing properly. Your doctor will make a note of these pre-conditions and state that you were more vulnerable because you were already suffering some form of illness or disability. However, with this knowledge, ongoing problems or ones that develop later, which seem unrelated to your accident, can be quickly addressed.

Tell your doctor everything. Tell him if your pain continues or worsens, if you have sleep problems, if you are gaining or losing weight or if you have any problems with your appetite or bowels.

Roy

Roy was lucky that his friend Jackson had time, in the weeks following the accident, to drive him to the physiotherapist and to the clinics to have X-rays and other tests. Roy took his doctor's advice, followed through with all recommended treatments and kept notes on everything.

Two years after the accident, Roy had made a good recovery and moved to settle his claim through mediation.

When Jackson met with him after the mediation hearing, he asked, "So, how did you make out, buddy?"

Roy grimaced. "Good enough, but not great. At least it's finally settled. But dealing with that claim was tough. I should really have taken that ambulance."

CHAPTER 12

Chronic Pain Syndrome

Luke

Luke was looking to make up for lost time. After three years in prison and another on parole, he was finally out from under his parole officer's constant snooping. Now he just wanted to get back on his hog and ride with the boys.

After downing five beers at a roadside pub and snorting two lines of cocaine in the pub's men's room, Luke was having trouble with the zipper on his leather jacket.

"Need some help with that, big guy?" Jerry, his riding partner, slurred at him as they joined the twenty other black leather clad gang members assembling by the row of motorcycles.

The roar of the men revving their motorcycles shattered the quiet of the mountainside town. The pub owner was always glad to see them, but the locals were just as happy to see them leave.

Luke was their leader and they fell in behind him and Jerry along the highway. As they came up behind a logging truck making its way to the mill down the highway, Jerry waved, cautioning Luke to fall back.

Luke's vision was off, distorted by alcohol and cocaine. He didn't think he was tailgating. He waved his buddy off.

Just then, the logging truck braked heavily, trying to avoid hitting a boulder that had fallen onto the road.

Unable to react in time, Luke slammed into the back of the truck. He and his Harley slid under the rear axle of the truck as the driver continued to brake. Jerry swerved around the back corner of the truck and rolled into the ditch. Luke was dragged for another forty feet before the truck came to a stop. He tried to roll out from under the truck, but his legs were useless. He was writhing in pain as his buddies began to pull. They knew they shouldn't move him, but they had to get him out from under the vehicle. Someone called for an ambulance.

Luke was taken to the nearest hospital, where he was diagnosed with a compression fracture of his lower spine which caused severe back pain and made both his legs numb. After one month in hospital, he returned home in a wheelchair. Occupational and then rehabilitation therapists worked with him at home.

His doctor prescribed pain relievers, but Luke preferred beer and cocaine — he even sold his Harley to pay for his drugs. He became severely depressed.

His physician told him he had a chronic pain disorder, and referred him to a pain disorder clinic and a drug and alcohol addiction centre, both of which were covered by his provincial health plan.

Luke became reclusive. He refused to speak to his pregnant girlfriend or even to answer the phone. He kept his blinds closed and wouldn't answer the door. One day, his buddies broke down the door and found Luke in bed, unshaven, dirty, depressed and suicidal.

They took him to the pain clinic and got him referred to a psychiatrist, which is where I met him. Luke told me that he couldn't work after the accident, and complained that he couldn't even have sex. He explained that his Harley had been his last hope for fun in life, and that his girlfriend was always complaining that all he did was bellyache about his problems.

I filled out a prescription for antidepressants, and suggested he look at the situation from a more positive perspective — that he had survived what could have very easily been a fatal accident, that he was going to be a father and that, by going to a pain clinic and seeing a psychiatrist, he was taking steps to improve his situation.

Luke continued to refill his prescriptions every month. His major sorrow continued to be the loss of his bike, more even than the chronic pain and inability to walk.

Chronic pain syndrome

Everyone feels pain. It is a useful and necessary sensation. It tells you that you have an injury or illness and you should do something about it. But chronic pain is pain that is persistent and long-lasting, often more than three to six months. Pain is both difficult to explain the cause of and to diagnose. It can be fatiguing and psychologically draining. It can be disabling and has the potential to affect all aspects of your life. Some complaints include lower levels of confidence, chronic fatigue, anxiety or even severe depression. Hot packs, rubbing gels and other over-the-counter remedies can help provide temporary relief, but you probably need more effective long-lasting prescriptions and treatments.

It will be important for you to be assertive in getting help. Be proactive in helping yourself and following through with suggested therapies from your physician. For example, keep a day-to-day record of your pain so you can understand and better explain your condition. This can help you understand what works to improve your condition and what doesn't. Talk to your physician about a referral to either a specialist or a centre that specializes in chronic pain. Keep moving, stay as active as possible and, on the advice of your physician, get into an exercise routine.

Chronic pain disorder clinics

Chronic pain clinics are now present in most of the larger cities in Canada. These are a relatively new idea, bringing together a number of different types of specialists in a single setting. This generally includes a team of medical doctors, social workers, psychiatrists, psychologists and both occupational and rehabilitation specialists. You will need to be referred by a physician to receive treatment in one of these clinics. Some private pain clinics may be covered by your medical plan or your insurance policy.

Such clinics educate you about your injury, as well of the possible causes of and methods of dealing with your pain. They might offer you different rehabilitation methods, psychological self-management skills, exercises, medications or a combination of these. If your pain did not get better with earlier treatments, the clinic may suggest more intensive therapies. Your spouse or family might also be involved at various points throughout your treatments — they can be more help to you if they understand what you are going through.

Chronic pain and depression

Chronic pain may be so long-lasting and disabling that patients become depressed and anxious. They might begin to avoid social and family gatherings, or even become addicted to alcohol or drugs. Depression and anxiety disorders are real medical conditions and help is available.

Medications

You may receive a number of medications, which you would take in combination. These could include either over-the-counter or prescription muscle relaxants, anti-inflammatory medications or painkillers. People suffering from depression as well as chronic pain find that some of the newer antidepressant medications taken together with an anticonvulsant have been very helpful in suppressing pain. Medical marijuana is still controversial, but is prescribed by certain doctors and some pain clinics.

The holistic approach

This is an idea where the 'whole person', so to speak, is looked at. This approach can include the physical, nutritional, environmental, emotional, social, spiritual and other lifestyle aspects. It may also include alternative medicine, which may involve treatments that are not recognized by classical medical schools. These include treatments such as homeopathy, acupuncture, vitamin and dietary supplements, yoga and hypnosis.

Remember, this book is not recommending any form of treatment. In it, I am attempting only to inform you, to educate you about what may be available in your community. You should always discuss any alternative pain treatments with your regular doctor, who understands your specific conditions. Mixing medications of any type might be problematic as negative side effects could arise.

Be cautious!!

Luke

Eight years after the settlement, Luke's wife called me for an opinion about one of their sons who school counselors had diagnosed as hyperactive. I asked about Luke.

She told me that after the accident, before their marriage and the birth of their twins, he had started swimming almost every day, lost forty pounds and joined the Toastmasters speaking group. He now gives lectures on addiction and motorcycle safety to students at the local schools. She told me, "He will always be in a wheelchair. But he's become an excellent public speaker, and even the national president of Toastmasters! He's never been happier, doctor," she added, "And he's a good husband to me and a great dad to our boys."

I suspect he was such a good speaker to the students because he used his own rough-and-ready tough jargon rather than lecturing to them.

Don't just sit back and wait. Don't give up. Be proactive. Even after a debilitating accident, you may still be able to exercise: swim, walk or play a gentle game of golf. But always on the advice of your physician.

CHAPTER 13

Whiplash Injuries

Ahmad

The highway was busy and the rain was coming down in sheets as everyone rushed to get home that evening.

'We don't need more rain, that's for sure,' Ahmad thought. He was tired and hungry after a hard day's work as a longshoreman, plus working overtime. His windshield wipers were on high, but they didn't really help.

He drove in the fast lane, just under the speed limit, and shook his head at the number of single-occupancy cars in the High Occupancy Vehicle (HOV) lane. Then he noticed a BMW behind him swerving in and out of different lanes on the five-lane freeway.

"All that just to get ahead by a few car lengths," Ahmad muttered. "Stupid."

Ahmad slowed down. The bridge ahead was always a bottleneck. Approaching it, traffic generally slowed considerably, but he had already anticipated the problem and was ready when the car in front of him braked sharply.

He heard what sounded like an explosion, and felt his Mazda lurch forward into the back of the Malibu ahead of him. The collision propelled his head forward and then back against the headrest with such force that he briefly lost consciousness.

The kid from the BMW woke him up by banging on the window. He was angry and threatening. "Why did you slow down, pinhead?" the kid shouted, pointing at his front bumper. "Look! My bumper. See!"

Ahmad rolled down his window. 'Why was this kid shouting at me?', he wondered. He was still stunned. He held the back of his neck and felt nauseous.

The woman driving the Malibu walked back, worried about Ahmad. She called the police. Traffic slowed down to a crawl, but no one else stopped to help.

When the police cars arrived, they found Ahmad sitting on the side of the road, confused and holding his head in his hands. They pulled his car and the Malibu off the road, but the BMW had gone. The paramedics put Ahmad in a neck brace, strapped his body to a stretcher and took him to the hospital. He was examined for severe whiplash.

The emergency room doctors examined Ahmad and gave him a prescription for pain relievers. They discharged him with a neck brace for comfort.

The pain did not go away and Ahmad continued to complain of unrelenting neck pain, which was worse whenever he turned his head. He had headaches, shooting pains into his shoulders and stiffness in his upper back. He couldn't sleep without pills.

After a few weeks of rest and recuperation, Ahmad was feeling somewhat better. He was able to manage without the neck brace. Because he couldn't turn his head without shooting pains down his shoulders, he couldn't return to work and his doctor placed him on short-term disability and ordered physiotherapy and massage therapy.

This type of injury to the neck is referred to as a cervical sprain, cervical strain or hyperextension injury, but whiplash is the non-medical term used to describe specific types of damage to the upper spine resulting in neck pain. This might occur following an injury to the bones, ligaments, tendons and muscles in your neck.

It is one of the most common physical injuries in motor vehicle accidents. Whiplash may cause a period of disability. Some people have stiffness, pain and a lack of movement for a period of time after the injury. These symptoms may be more pronounced in the elderly, especially to those with pre-existing arthritic conditions or previously healed injuries in the upper back or neck, but children are also susceptible.

Symptoms may include:
- pain and stiffness or tenderness in the back or sides of the neck
- muscle spasms in your back or neck
- difficulty moving your head
- headaches
- dizziness
- jaw pain

Whiplash-associated disorder may describe a version of whiplash with a more severe and chronic condition in which the nerves coming out of the spinal cord may have been damaged by being pulled and bruised in the injury. In more severe cases of this disorder, there may be arm and shoulder paralysis in addition to the other problems listed above.

Whiplash may happen after a rear-ender, when your head suddenly moves forward and then snaps back. This may cause damage as your head and neck are forced beyond their normal range of motion. When your car is struck from behind, the seat pushes your body forward into the seatbelt, but your head and neck jerk backwards. Your head can then be thrown into a forward position again, with your neck ending up in an S-shape — the ligaments, tendons and small muscles that hold your neck bones together may be strained, pulled, twisted, sprained and injured.

If emergency responders suspect whiplash or a spinal injury, they may place a cervical collar around your neck and strap you to a spinal board. This prevents movement and further injuries while you are being transferred to a hospital for further assessment. As soon as possible, follow up with your own physician. Your doctor will be able to monitor your condition and progress, will recommend treatment options and, if necessary, order further tests. The doctor may also instruct you about continued use of a cervical collar should one be required.

Treatment of whiplash

Exercise, manual therapy, pain medication, muscle relaxants and other therapies are all very helpful for whiplash injuries. Your family physician and other consultants may offer more therapeutic suggestions, which will be important for you to follow.

How to prevent whiplash

Always use seat belts and ensure that head restraints are properly set to limit the potential for injury. Read your car manual and follow the directions as to seat settings. Most newer automobiles have air-bags and air curtains to further protect you from injury. It is very important to follow the instructions in your car manual and advice from proper authorities as to child seat restraints and booster seats.

Ahmad

Three months after the accident, Ahmad had completed his physiotherapy and massage treatments. He could now turn his head without pain and was able to drive again. He returned to work within a few months. He remained apprehensive about driving for some time after his accident, especially in the rain and on that same stretch of freeway.

"I'm ninety percent better and I'm back at work," Ahmad told his doctor soon after. "Thanks for the prescription, but I don't need those pills anymore."

CHAPTER 14

Traumatic Brain Injury (TBI) (or Neurocognitive Disorders) and Post-Concussion Syndrome (PCS)

Elsie

"Good evening, Elsie."

"Nice day, wasn't it, Elsie?"

"How are you today, Elsie?"

Everyone at the bus stop knew Elsie and she knew everyone there that late afternoon. She'd lost her hearing aid last week, but she could still see their lips moving. She nodded and smiled to everyone.

"Where's your hearing aid, Elsie?" Freddy, her next-door neighbour, shouted while pointing at his ear.

"What'd you say, Freddy? Glasses?" Elsie replied sheepishly. "Oh my, my. Sat on them, sat on them. Silly me." She pushed her walker to the front of the line as the bus approached.

Everyone stood back patiently as they waited for the bus driver to lower the ramp. Elsie slowly maneuvered her walker and then her frail body onto the bus.

"Good evening, Elsie. Take your time," the driver said. "Not far to the end of the line," he added reassuringly.

That's where Elsie lived. At the end of the line, alone, without family and with only a tattered picture album to remind her of days gone by. Her son had left her there in a rented basement suite last year. He never came back to see her.

Elsie sat at the front of the bus, in the seniors' area. The wire cage on her walker was full of groceries. She was getting more and more weary from her daily outings.

It wasn't long before the bus slowed and pulled into the terminal. The driver waited patiently as Elsie got up slowly and pushed her walker off the ramp.

"Goodnight, Elsie. Take good care now, you hear?" the driver said.

Elsie didn't hear but she nodded, knowing that he had said something to her. She moved her walker to the crosswalk between the bus stalls and began crossing to the opposite sidewalk, which led straight to her house. It was always safe to do this in the terminal as the buses alternated every quarter-hour.

But not this time.

"Elsie, don't go," the driver shouted, jumping up from his seat. "Stop, Elsie. Stop!"

Elsie didn't hear. And she didn't see the four teenagers in a SUV pulling in to make an illegal U-turn in the bus depot. They sideswiped the bus and plowed into Elsie and her walker. Groceries went flying, people screamed, the bus driver ran to her side. The SUV took off, leaving Elsie lying unconscious in a heap.

Suddenly, everyone was giving orders about not moving her, about calling the police, fire department and an ambulance. Elsie was finally taken to the local hospital.

Elsie was in a coma for three days. She had a broken hip and broken ribs. For the next six months, Elsie, now in a seniors' low-cost residential care home, complained of severe headaches. She couldn't remember her old address or her son's name and her speech was garbled. Neurological tests showed that she had suffered a traumatic brain injury, or TBI, also referred to as a neurocognitive disorder.

Traumatic brain injury and post-concussion syndrome

Traumatic brain injury (TBI), now referred to as a neurocognitive disorder, and the more serious post-concussion syndrome (PCS), refer to head injuries in which the brain has been damaged by a blow to the head. Quite simply, either disorder may be caused by a blunt-force trauma, or blow, to the head, which may result in the blood vessels inside your brain being bruised or broken. It has been described as the brain's equivalent of a black eye. Such a disorder might also be the result of Alzheimer's, substance abuse, infection or other conditions, but here it will be applied only to motor vehicle traumas.

The damage to the blood vessels in the brain can produce a subdural hematoma, or bleeding, under the dura, which is a membrane sheath separating your brain from the inner skull. This bleeding could potentially increase the pressure within your skull, putting pressure on the brain and causing many additional short or long-term neurological problems.

The diagnosis may be made on the initial examination, by the ambulance crew, in the ER or later, by your family physician. Depending on the severity of the injury, you might need more extensive neurological examinations. Once a diagnosis is made, the ER doctor or your family doctor may refer you to a neurologist, a neurosurgeon, a psychiatrist or a neuropsychologist, who will further assess and treat the major problems.

Some possible symptoms of TBI and PCS:
- severe headaches
- nausea
- vomiting
- dizziness
- serious memory problems
- concentration problems
- a reoccurring sense of confusion

Some possible physical problems of TBI:
- paralysis of the limbs
- problems with eye sight
- problems with hearing
- memory or concentration difficulties

There may be further possible psychological problems such as the development of:
- anxiety
- depression
- behavioural disorders (such as anger, irritability or aggression)

Using the Glasgow Coma Scale to grade a patient's level of consciousness, doctors and paramedics classify head injuries as mild, moderate or severe. This scale is used by medical practitioners to communicate the degree of a patient's injury among themselves. They rate the person on a scale of 3 to 15 based on verbal, motor and eye-opening reactions to stimuli. A high score indicates spontaneous eye-opening, normal conversation and normal motor response, while a lower score suggests a lack of consciousness or functionality. That is: a Glasgow Coma Scale of 13 or above indicates a mild head injury, 9–12 suggests a moderate injury, 8 or below indicates a more severe injury. The scale also provides a baseline to observe a patient's progress as treatment progresses.

Treatments depend on the severity of the TBI. Severe injuries and coma may need intensive care on a neurological ward and could require surgery. Even less severe injuries might require hospitalization with mild sedation to keep the patient quiet so the brain can heal. Most individuals with mild TBI generally recover within a few months, but this will depend on many factors, which are best explained by a family physician. In mild cases the symptoms should gradually clear up after a few weeks. However, if the accident victim was severely injured and continued to have ongoing problems, he might be referred to a rehabilitation hospital or clinic with neurologists and other health care pro-fessionals who are specifically trained to treat brain injuries. I talk about many of these specialties in other chapters. Age, use of alcohol or drugs and previous head injuries can also hinder your recovery.

Your family physician might be able to give you more information on your specific disorder and recovery.

Elsie

Poor Elsie wasn't as lucky as most people with TBIs, who generally get better after a few months in recovery. A year later, she couldn't feed herself without assistance, was always getting lost and would be found walking about naked. She also became aggressive and hostile, swearing at the nurses and other residents.

The visiting doctor diagnosed her post-concussion syndrome. The long-term prognosis was not good. Her recovery was not helped by her advanced age, fragile heart, high blood pressure, arteriosclerosis or the pain from the broken hip and ribs that never healed properly due to osteoporosis.

Post-concussion syndrome

Post-concussion syndrome is a head injury that may be more severe and incapacitating than traumatic brain disorder. This was once known as 'shell shock', following wartime trauma and injuries. The complaints generally last longer than TBI and may be more disabling due to a more severe physical injury to the brain. PCS can be accompanied by major physical, cognitive, emotional and behavioural problems that make it unlikely the patient will be able to look after themselves, maintain employment or be socially involved. Many sufferers of PCS need support and care from family, friends and physicians until they have sufficiently recovered. This might also include bringing in occupational and rehabilitation therapists to assist with coping and to spur recovery on.

If you are diagnosed with TBI or a post-concussional disorder, your family and friends may well become caregivers until you recover. The loss of former lifestyle and stress upon relationships can produce problems and household tension. In these cases, each member of the household could benefit from education and counseling to help them deal with any long-term changes, and to support one another.

Recovery might take a long time, so it is important to be brave and have strong faith in yourself. You might recall stories about courageous artists, actors, musicians, soldiers or athletes who have gone through months and years of therapy following brain injuries. With desire and dedication, many patients are able to overcome their disabilities and to once again become highly functioning individuals. With willpower and a drive to overcome the situation, you may be able to do the same.

Elsie

Unfortunately, Elsie never recovered. Her advanced age and many medical and orthopedic issues prevented it. She needed full-time care in the senior's home.

The visiting doctor convinced her son to visit. They found her standing in her doorway naked, talking to herself. The doctor took off his white coat, covered her frail body and led her back into her room. The doctor turned to talk to her son but he was already walking away.

CHAPTER 15

Post-Traumatic Stress Disorder (PTSD)

Miguel

Miguel felt his heart pounding with excitement as the bus pulled up to the stop. He was on his way to the airport to meet his elderly parents who were arriving from Manila. He hadn't seen them since they had arranged for him to escape the violence of his homeland in his youth. After working in a number of countries, he was now safe in Vancouver with two children and an ex-wife.

He climbed aboard and dropped the fare into the ticket box. He asked the driver, "This bus will get me to somewhere I can get an airport connection?"

"Yes sir," the driver assured him. "This bus will take you to the SkyTrain, and that will take you directly to the airport." Miguel gripped the overhead strap with one hand as other passengers jostled by him, pushing him to the rear.

At each stop, a small crowd pushed past him, getting on and off. As the bus slowly started forward, he let go of the strap for a moment and turned towards the back of the bus. He didn't see the small car dart out in front of the bus.

The bus driver slammed on the brakes. Miguel lost his footing and was thrown towards the front of the bus.

Miguel grabbed at the hand railing to try to stop his fall. But he missed it and went down, smashing his head on the edge of the steel fare box.

Miguel was knocked out. He doesn't know how long. He thinks he remembers hearing someone shouting, but he couldn't see anything and his ears were ringing. His next real memory was the tight cuff on his arm, a siren wailing somewhere in the distance and the ambulance paramedics talking to him as they wheeled him through the ER doors into the hospital.

"Blood pressure's stable. He's coming around."

Miguel suffered from disturbing and distressing recollections and dreams about the accident and past events that repeated over and over after he regained his memory. He felt anxious all the time and his head ached. He would break out in a rash. His muscles felt tense and his heart raced. He was often short of breath, and he developed stomach problems. His interest in sex just about disappeared.

He also began to lose weight, and complained to his doctor of diarrhea. Miguel felt exhausted all the time and became very depressed. His nightmares were horrific — he kept having flashbacks of riding a bus that was flipping over or on fire or careening off a cliff. His concentration was affected, his memory was poor and he couldn't focus or multitask. He felt a constant sense of anxiety and a fear of reliving the near-death experience.

Miguel suffered from post-traumatic stress disorder for the next two years, which was complicated by his earlier traumatic experiences witnessing severe brutality and death in his former country. During this time, he tried to avoid any thoughts of the accident. His parents had returned to the Philippines after staying with him for several months. They were supportive during his recovery, but he wouldn't talk about the accident to his family or friends. He avoided using public transit and became housebound, introverted and isolated. When he did talk about it, he became panicky and twice ended up in emergency complaining of a heart attack.

He still had some time to go before his medical-legal claim might be settled. By this time he was $60,000 in debt. His *credit cards were maxed, his bank loan payments were due and his line of credit was coming to an end.*

Financially, he was now dependent on his friends, having cashed in his RRSPs and an old insurance policy as he continued trying to help his ex-wife and to support his children as best as he could.

His lawyer told him that a psychiatrist he had seen for an IME had reported back that he was suffering from post-traumatic stress and had suggested that Miguel seek treatment.

Post-traumatic stress disorder

If you have been in or even witnessed an accident that involved death, injury or a threat to either yourself or another person, you might develop some or all the symptoms and complaints of post-traumatic stress disorder, or PTSD. Those suffering from PTSD can experience frightening memories, have flashbacks of the accident, have nightmares that wake them in a panic, experience daytime anxiety or have depression related to the traumatic event.

If you are experiencing these problems, you should see your family physician as soon as possible. Your doctor will either treat you or refer you to others for therapy. If you do not seek treatment, PTSD could potentially interfere with your daily activities and your ability to have or maintain relationships with others. It could lead to long-term disability. PTSD can be acute if your complaints last less than six months, or it may be called chronic if it lasts six months or longer.

Many people experience this disorder. For example, some soldiers or civilian non-combatants have similar reactions after witnessing or being party to horrific experiences. Personal injury, being diagnosed with cancer or a chronic disorder, a sexual assault or natural disasters like earthquakes may also induce a post-traumatic stress response. There are often support groups for those involved in major disasters or similar situations. A family physician, local medical or mental health clinics or your computer may be accessed for information on individual help or support groups.

Some possible symptoms of PTSD:
- frightening memories of the traumatic event
- extreme fear
- feelings of helplessness, horror and hopelessness
- nightmares
- flashbacks
- heart racing or palpitations
- shortness of breath
- sweating
- feeling faint

Other possible symptoms might include avoiding thoughts or conversations with other people about the accident or avoiding people, places or activities that remind the sufferer of the event.

Thinking and behaviour may change. A person with PTSD may experience some of the following:
- faulty memory
- poor concentration
- irritability
- anger or aggression

Mood changes may occur, to the point of suffering with some of the following:
- severe depression
- crying episodes
- loss of interest in everything
- sexual problems
- sleep disturbance

Other disorders associated with PTSD:
- panic disorders
- phobias (strong unnatural fears, such as fear of enclosed places)

- obsessive-compulsive habits (hand-washing many times a day, or other new rituals)
- social phobias (such as fear of seeing others)
- depressive disorders
- addiction to drugs or alcohol

PTSD can occur at any age, including childhood. The extent and severity of PTSD and the person's vulnerability might depend on what kind of social support he has, family history, past traumatic experiences and past medical and psychological history.

If caught in the early stages, PTSD may be treated by a family physician, but you may need more help from consultants and therapists. A family physician may refer you to therapists, hospitals or group therapy clinics. Psychiatric treatments are covered by medical plans, if referral is by a family doctor. Private insurance may cover therapists, psychologists or other types of counselors. Otherwise, the patient has to pay.

Counseling with a therapist or psychologist can produce excellent results. Family counseling is beneficial in that it helps family understand how to help the patient. Having a positive attitude and supportive family and friends is often a great help and very therapeutic. Medications such as tension relievers, sleeping sedatives, or mild antidepressants can be helpful in dealing with PTSD.

If you yourself have PTSD symptoms and your family physician or lawyer refers you to a psychiatrist, don't be frightened. The psychiatrist may prescribe more specific medication, which may reduce the disturbing symptoms described in previous paragraphs. The medication may help you manage the panic, depression or severe anxiety, and you may get out more, be more active and less socially isolated. You may be able to think more clearly, be more hopeful, more decisive and, possibly, return to work sooner.

If you see a psychologist, he or she will most likely use cognitive therapy approaches. This type of treatment may encourage you toward more positive thinking, a better approach when dealing with the trauma and your complaints.

Don't wait. Get help immediately. See your doctor. Get treatment quickly. Accept referrals to qualified consultants and other therapists like psychologists and psychiatrists. On your physician's advice, get up and start being active. You will get better faster with treatment.

Miguel

Miguel developed chronic PTSD, but he did get therapy and he did get better. He saw a psychologist, a psychiatrist and a rehabilitation worker, who assisted him in his return to work.

He saw his psychologist weekly for long-term cognitive therapy, which taught him how to relax, think positively, plan ahead and set new goals. She encouraged him to see his friends.

Throughout his treatment he was able to travel, find new work and establish a healthy relationship with a young woman, after his divorce.

The psychiatrist saw him often and prescribed medication to calm him down, give him a good night's sleep and stop his nightmares and flashbacks.

CHAPTER 16

Anxiety, Panic Attacks
and Panic Disorders

David

It was only a small accident, so calling the police or ambulance didn't seem necessary, but it was still a shocking experience for David, a man in his mid-thirties. He had stopped his car at a crosswalk and was daydreaming about his girlfriend when a taxi van making a right-hand turn slid into his front left fender. David was shocked to see the taxi's heavy grille in his face. Immediately, he felt panicked by the unexpected lurch and the noise of grinding metal.

Once David's heart stopped thumping, he tried to catch his breath. He got out of his car to survey the damage and told a passerby, who was about to call the police, "No, no police. No one's injured. There's no need."

After exchanging phone numbers and insurance information with the taxi driver, who was very polite and very sorry, David drove away, physically unharmed. But three days later, when his boss asked him to drive across town to make a special delivery, he felt the panic well up again.

When he got into his car with the package, he broke into a sweat. His hands were so sweaty and clammy he couldn't grip the steering wheel. His heart was racing, he was gasping for breath, his stomach was in his throat — he got the door open just in time to vomit his breakfast onto the parking lot.

For months after, David suffered from severe headaches and nausea. He couldn't drive to unfamiliar places or anywhere outside his immediate community. His boss had to find someone else to make those deliveries. David even felt nervous if he was a passenger in his friends' cars. He would hold on tight to the door handle and feel dizzy. He was always asking friends who were driving to "Take it easy" or "Please, slow down."

After a while, he just stopped seeing friends. He drank beer, smoked two packs a day and stayed home to play games on his computer.

After several weeks of this, David's mother became very worried. She suggested he see his family doctor.

"Are you kidding, Ma?" David replied, lighting up another cigarette and downing his third beer of the morning, trying to relax. "He'll think I'm crazy. No way,"

That small accident was enough to set off a series of terrifying panic attacks whenever David drove his car or was a passenger in a vehicle outside familiar surroundings.

Anxiety, panic attacks and panic disorders

Some very common anxiety disorders after a traumatic motor vehicle accident include panic attacks, or panic disorders, and general anxiety disorders. These can include social phobias such as agoraphobia, a condition where there is a deep fear of public places or crowds.

General anxiety and panic attacks

A panic attack is a sudden surge of overwhelming fear. It can come without warning and is much more than just being stressed-out or nervous. During a panic attack, a person might feel a pounding of the heart, sweating, shortness of breath or a feeling of choking.

Some people experience feelings of being unreal, fear that they are going crazy, are having a heart attack or are dying. These sensations generally pass after a few minutes, but frequent attacks may continue for a long time.

Diagnosing panic attacks

The diagnosis is generally based on the following complaints or symptoms. Be aware, however, that these can differ from person to person:

- palpitations
- pounding in the chest
- sudden or excessive sweating
- trembling
- shortness of breath
- feelings of being detached from reality
- feelings of choking
- chills or hot flashes
- feelings of numbness or tingling sensations anywhere in the body
- chest pain
- nausea
- dizziness or feeling faint
- fear of losing control
- fear of going crazy
- fear of dying

Sufferers of general anxiety and panic disorders might see a number of doctors before being diagnosed. Many end up rushing to the emergency room, convinced they are having a heart attack. A doctor may order many tests in order to confirm it's not a coronary problem. Women, most commonly between the ages of twenty to forty-five, are more prone to panic attacks than men. Many sufferers of panic attacks become depressed because of the uncertainty of what is happening to them, seeing so many physicians and waiting for so many tests. Most therapists believe that inheritance, close relatives with anxiety problems and genetics are important factors in causing panic attacks.

The first attack might be triggered by a minor fender-bender or worries about a medical problem. Any major life stress: surgery, pregnancy or even coffee, tea and some stimulating medications can contribute to setting off a panic attack. Street drugs such as speed, LSD, marijuana and cocaine, alcohol and some antidepressants can also be very stimulating to the nervous system and might trigger an attack. Complications can develop in some patients who become agoraphobic, that is, afraid of being out in public or dealing with crowds. In these cases, sufferers tend to isolate themselves, to shun family and friends and be more prone to alcohol or drug abuse and depression.

Treatment

If you have a panic attack, remember, you are not alone. See your physician and then a therapist, perhaps a psychiatrist or a psychologist. Remind yourself that you will not die and that you are not crazy. Calm yourself down with deep breathing. Relax your muscles, take deep breaths, hold them and then let your breath out slowly as if you are blowing out a candle. Try to get some exercise every day, something that you enjoy doing.

Talk to your doctor. She might be able to offer you a prescription to calm your nerves. If you are not improving, she can refer you to a therapist such as a psychiatrist or a qualified psychologist who can help you get better. Dealing with all of this can be difficult, but keep in mind that suffering from panic is a very common disorder, and that it is treatable.

Anxiety disorder and social phobia

Simply put, anxiety is a medical term for nervousness. Anxiety can cause symptoms such as heart pounding, nausea, shortness of breath and a feeling of tightness in the muscles, especially in the neck and shoulders. These sensations are similar to sensations during panic attacks, but they can last all day and for a very long time. A panic attack is a shorter-lasting fear, with relative comfort in between attacks, while those with an anxiety disorder can have the feeling of anxiety and fear all the time.

Common physical and emotional concerns

Anxiety disorders can cause all of the same physical concerns as those listed under panic attacks, but they can be ongoing, with constant ups and downs in severity. Until treated, there can be ongoing problems such as shortness of breath, stomach problems, heart palpitations and general nervousness or emotional problems like being afraid, apprehension, inability to concentrate, irritability, short-temperedness or even depression.

Treatment

Get help as soon as possible! If you believe you are suffering from anxiety, see your physician and get a thorough medical check-up. Your doctor might examine your thyroid, which can cause anxiety if it is overactive, and may also check for low blood sugar, heart problems, infections or asthma, or other conditions — all of which may trigger anxiety. Tell him what over-the-counter medications, herbal remedies and recreational drugs you're taking. They, too, may sometimes precipitate anxiety attacks. Once these possible causes are dismissed, the next step should be to see a therapist, such as a psychologist or psychiatrist, who may work with you often and regularly.

Generally, anxiety disorders are treated by a psychologist with cognitive behavioural therapy. Or you may be prescribed medication from either a psychiatrist, your family doctor or both. For more about cognitive behaviour therapy, see chapter on psychologists and treatments.

Social anxiety disorder and social phobia

Social anxiety disorder or social phobia is the fear of being scrutinized, judged or embarrassed in public. Some people are afraid that others will think badly of them and therefore feel anxious. This anxiety generally diminishes when at home, away from social situations. It's very common, especially in women. Social anxiety can also be triggered by a threat or illness, or it may follow a bout of panic or a motor vehicle accident, causing overwhelming stress and frightening chaos.

Many people experience social anxiety when they feel as if they are 'on stage'. This is a common condition known as generalized social anxiety disorder in which patients avoid speaking to strangers, socializing, going out to restaurants, speaking publicly or even using public washrooms. Physical problems can include intense blushing, sweating, hot flushes, shortness of breath, nausea, vomiting and diarrhea. Some sufferers notice their hands tremble, especially at the table, or experience heart palpitations and chest pains. Others find themselves feeling like they have to urinate. Friends may complain that those with social anxiety or phobias become too dependent on their friends and that they won't go out alone. Some patients become dependent on alcohol or street drugs in an attempt to calm themselves down.

Coping with social anxiety and social phobia

- sit down and try to understand where all this is coming from
- learn to control your breathing and relax your muscles

- cut down on caffeinated drinks, alcohol, cigarettes and other stimulants
- learn about meditation, yoga, muscle stretching and relaxation techniques
- get into a physical exercise program or a social anxiety group
- see your doctor and get some medication to calm you down so that you can think more clearly
- get a referral to a therapist, physiotherapist or psychologist
- have faith in yourself

Remember, these are relatively common problems that can be overcome. If encountering difficulties, see your physician and possibly a therapist. Try to exercise every day, something physical that you enjoy doing.

David

Do you remember what David said when his mother told him to see a psychiatrist as his physician recommended? He said, "Are you kidding, Ma? He'll think I'm crazy. No way."

Well, David's mom is a very persuasive woman. She soon convinced David to see a therapist. He saw the specialist once a week and found that he felt calmer talking about his fears just after the accident and about the stress he was under at work. He told her about his girlfriend, who worked as a taxi dispatcher and was pressuring him to get married, which turned out to be his major dilemma and fear-inducer.

The bump from the taxi may have brought on David's fear of marriage!

David began taking prescription medication for anxiety and a sleeping sedative. His therapist referred him to a qualified psychologist who taught David how to relax with cognitive therapy, how to deal with his stresses and how to resolve his fears about marriage.

David worked through his anxiety and panic problems, and was no longer isolated. He stopped using alcohol as a means to calm himself down and he quit smoking. After a few months of therapy, he was again able to drive anywhere, was productive at work and was working to develop a closer relationship with his girlfriend.

CHAPTER 17

Depressive Disorders, Obsessive-Compulsive Disorders and Drug and Alcohol Addiction

Lucas

It was eight a.m. when Lucas pulled out his stash from the loose floorboard under his carpet. He had time to relax before his mother came home from her night shift at the hotel. She had lost interest in him and in life in general since his father's suicide two years ago.

He rolled a joint, and lit up while sending his only friend a text message to meet: "J & 12-30." Lucas knew he could get down the hill to the corner of Johnston Ave. and 12th Street in half an hour. He grinned, knowing that the Plan X Cheetah eight-inch skateboard he'd stolen from a rich kid last week would easily beat his friend down that winding street.

Lucas finished his joint, downed two capsules of his antidepressant and checked the bindings on his skateboard, six times. He washed his hands for the fourteenth time since awakening and headed out, locking the basement door. He put the key very carefully exactly six inches under the edge of the outside carpet and checked the door again. His mother would find the key when she got home from work later that morning.

The sun was up, the street was clear of traffic and the pavement was finally dry after two days of rain. Lucas rechecked the door and made a slight adjustment to the key's position under the carpet. He strapped on his kneepads, adjusted his helmet, shook off the medication's dizzying effect and pushed off down the steep hill.

'This Cheetah is the best,' he thought, as he swooped and swerved down the winding and twisting thoroughfare. There was only one traffic light to deal with, and he figured that would be easy. There were no cars on Sunday. He grinned as he sped down the hill at 20, maybe 25 miles per hour.

He saw the traffic light ahead turn yellow. He could make it, he was sure of that.

Lucas didn't make it. He went through that red light at maybe 30 miles an hour, straight into the side of a Honda Accord, just ahead of the driver's door. Lucas flipped over the hood of the car, landing on the other side, unconscious.

It was the priest in the Honda — on his way to the church that early Sunday morning — who called 911.

Six months later Lucas had recovered from his soft-tissue neck injuries. His right leg, which had been fractured in three places, was still weak and required a knee brace. But it was healing reasonably well. Despite the fact he'd been wearing a helmet at the time of the accident, he had a serious concussion, which had negatively affected his memory and concentration.

Lucas was already suffering from depression after his father's death and became even more depressed because of his physical limitations and damaged memory. His repetitive behaviours increased: he now washed his hands 140 to 150 times a day. His hands were red and raw, but he had little time for or interest in actually bathing or showering.

He could no longer skateboard, and his only friend had found someone else to skateboard with. His rehabilitation consultant diagnosed him with a major depressive illness, an obsessive-compulsive disorder and substance-dependence.

She noted that there was a family history of depression, and recommended a referral to a psychiatrist.

Lucas had an obsessive or compulsive personality. He had always felt the compulsion to check up on things and had washed his hands excessively even before the mishap. But these were made much worse by the trauma, the anxiety and the stress in his life brought on by the accident.

Depressive disorders, obsessive-compulsive disorders and drug and alcohol addiction

Following a motor vehicle accident, almost everyone feels sadness and anger. This is normal. Almost everyone feels grief or bereavement when there is a major loss such as the death of a loved one, the end of a relationship or the loss of a limb. Bereavement may go on for a very long time, sometimes for many years. Following a motor vehicle accident, many victims react with anger or fear, particularly if they have been disfigured or disabled. Many are upset at the other driver for causing their disabilities — even if it wasn't the other driver's fault.

A feeling of deep sadness may take over as limitations progress, affecting a person's ability to function socially or at work. Intimate relationships may suffer, income drop and other losses continue to develop. With so many challenges, depression can become overwhelming.

Adjustment disorder with depressed mood

If you have a motor vehicle accident, you might be diagnosed with one of the common depressive disorders, referred to as an adjustment disorder with depressed mood. This is where the depression may have all of the symptoms and complaints of a depressive disorder, but is generally the result of overwhelming stress. Due to your physical and psychological limitations, you may not be able to cope with the medical-legal aspect of your MVA, the loss of employment or the loss of income. This can be compounded by increased stress in intimate relationships or other family difficulties.

This type of depressive disorder often clears up once the stressors are eliminated. However, psychological therapy or medication can help a patient get better faster. As patients begin feeling better with treatment, most are able to increase physical activity and return to work. Intimate relationships and the ability to socialize and pay off debts might also improve. As the various stressors are reduced, this type of depression may subside or disappear.

Some individuals develop a major depressive disorder within a short time after an accident. Stressors might not clear up. There could still be many physical and psychological limitations, continuing losses or there might have been a pre-existing depression or a family history of depression. In these cases, individuals can be more vulnerable to more serious types of depression.

Major depressive disorders

A major depressive disorder is just that — it is major. It can go on daily, constantly and consistently, with a sad mood. Severe depressions may be accompanied by episodes of crying, a sense of worthlessness, pessimism or feeling like a failure. Many people no longer enjoy the things they used to or feel guilty. Some feel they should be punished. There might be thoughts of severe self-criticism, restlessness, agitation or loss of interest combined with indecisiveness, feelings of worthlessness and loss of energy. Some sufferers are plagued by sleep disorders or develop an appetite disorder complete with the associated weight gain or loss. Others have difficulty with concentration and memory problems and could experience a serious loss of interest in intimate relationships and sexual activity. Some may be troubled with thoughts of suicide, and might even make the attempt.

Major depressive disorders can continue for a year or longer, but such disorders are treatable by your family physician, or with psychiatric and psychological therapy. Individuals suffering from such a major depressive disorder might be so overwhelmed by depression that they may not be able to function in their employment or in their home and personal life. They may be seriously disabled and be incapable of functioning socially. They stay at home, avoid interaction and become severely isolated, which may make the depression even worse.

Once again — if diagnosed, patients can recover from a major depression. Especially when treatment by a family doctor is combined with psychological therapy, psychiatric treatment with medication or group therapy.

Persistent depressive disorder or Dysthymic depressive disorder

Another form of depression is a persistent depressive disorder, previously known as a Dysthymic disorder. This is where a person suffers from a depressed mood most of the day and for most days. *Dysthymia* is a Greek word meaning despondency. It is a type of depression that might go on for many years, or even a lifetime. A person suffering from this type of chronic low-mood disorder might be able to function marginally or at a borderline level for many, many years. Feeling constantly low or having ongoing and consistent sadness can be troubling for both the sufferers and their families.

Family and friends might complain that those with this disorder seem down and despondent, even if they are able to get out, drive and interact. An ongoing low-mood disorder or sadness can be accompanied by a poor appetite, sleep disorders, fatigue, poor concentration and some disinterest in life. A motor vehicle accident can make Dysthymic depressive disorders worse. But the depression may not be as serious or as disabling as a major depressive disorder, or MDD. With MDD, you might be working hard to keep your head above water, but you may be able to continue to function. Sufferers with this type of depression can be helped by a family physician, a psychiatrist and by psychotherapy and medication.

Bipolar disorders

Bipolar disorder is a very different type of depression that can be precipitated by any type of trauma. It is characterized by a depressive or manic episode of bipolar illness, which is distinguished by shifts between episodes of hyperactivity, or mania, and depression. Some believe this type of disorder is genetic, or inherited, and that a depressive or manic episode of bipolar illness can be precipitated or hastened by any trauma, as in the case of a MVA.

Although there is some thinking that all forms of major depression and other disorders are caused by chemical imbalances in the brain, this has not been proved. The causes of these types of disorders are not yet fully understood. Heredity and genetics might have a direct cause in causing depression and in dictating a person's ability to deal with it.

Diagnosis of these types of depressive disorders might be made by a clinical interview with a family doctor, psychologist, psychiatrist or other consultants who a patient is seeing for other difficulties. One or another of these consultants may recognize that you are suffering from a depression and may indicate this verbally or in a written report, recommending a psychiatric evaluation. Your doctor or psychiatrist may give you other tests or something called the Beck Depression Inventory, which asks multiple questions about your state of depression. Responses to the questions will allow testers to grade depressions as mild, moderate or severe.

A patient may receive treatment for an adjustment disorder, a major depressive disorder, Dysthymic disorder or bipolar disorders from a registered professional counselor who can give emotional support. Additionally, medications might be required for an extended period, as might further long-term support and counseling with a qualified psychologist or a psychiatrist.

If a psychiatric evaluation does occur, the psychiatrist could recommend antidepressant or antianxiety medication, or other appropriate medication, together with a bedtime sedative. The purpose of these medications is to help deal with severe depression and promote clear thinking, which might help to motivate patients to get some exercise, be more socially active and gradually get back to work. If the person is suffering from a long-standing low-grade depression, such as the Dysthymic type or a bipolar disorder, antidepressants and other medications might be needed for an indefinite period of time.

If you are feeling down or sad and depressed and are having difficulty getting over it, you should see your family physician and get an evaluation. He may be able to help you with counseling during more extended visits or refer you to other therapists. He could prescribe medication or refer you to a psychologist for cognitive therapy or a psychiatrist for further consultation. Depressive disorders are treatable, and you will likely see improvement. It is important to be compliant, that is, to follow your physician's recommendations and stay on the prescribed medications. Do not stop taking them without first consulting with your doctor.

Obsessive-compulsive disorders

Many people have obsessive or compulsive personality traits. When a person's mind is absorbed with constant recurrent thoughts, these are called obsessions. When someone always checks up on things or cleans excessively, these are called compulsions. Some people have both obsessions and compulsions. Lucas had those compulsions before his accident, and they were probably made worse by the anxiety and stress brought on by the trauma of the accident. People with obsessive-compulsive disorders, or OCD, have uncontrollable and unwanted thoughts and/or repetitive behaviours. The obsessive aspect of OCD means having constant thoughts that one cannot turn off, while the compulsive aspect includes repetitive activities like the unconscious and repetitive washing of hands. These are psychological problems that can become disturbing and distracting in your lifestyle.

Aside from the frequent washing of hands, the compulsive examples of OCD can include constant cleaning or reorganizing, continually working to make sure everything in the house or office is in exactly the right place and very orderly. When others move or shift an object, sufferers of OCD might immediately feel the need to put it back in the right place. Some people with this condition are counters, needing to count items in every situation, while others need to check the same thing five, twenty, sixty times before they leave the house or office. Many are also very superstitious about numbers or colours.

Treatment for OCD is generally very effective, especially with ongoing cognitive behaviour therapy or medications like anti-depressants.

If you believe that you have been stricken with this type of disorder after the trauma of an accident, I urge you to see your family physician and get treatment.

Alcoholism and drug addictions

Addictions can also be common developments after a motor vehicle accident. People may find themselves self-medicating with alcohol or drugs to calm their fears, cope with stress or to reduce their anxiety or depression. Complications might arise because alcohol and drugs are addictive and, over time, the individual may require more and more to get the good effects. Additionally, substance abuse can contribute to other motor vehicle or workplace accidents or cause problems in interpersonal relationships, which might result in broken families or destroyed friendships.

Alcohol abusers and drug users commonly make excuses to drink alone and may become despondent with friends or family if confronted about their daily drinking or substance abuse. They might hide a stash or bottles. Many will stop eating and going out, while others will mix their medications with alcohol or other nonprescription drugs. Gradually they become disinterested in their appearance and turn irritable, aggressive and, possibly, belligerent.

As drug and alcohol consumption increases, thinking, talking and walking may become problematic. Hangovers, blackouts and other physical problems such as muscle weakness, liver problems, memory disorder and paralysis are all common amongst addicts and substance abusers. If treated, these problems may be remedied. If you have a substance abuse problem, listen to friends and family and admit you have a problem. See your family doctor and get a referral to a drug and alcohol treatment centre. Both psychologists and psychiatrists can be a great help to you and there are wonderful group therapy programs available. These include Alcoholics Anonymous and other treatment programs through local churches or community centres.

Lucas

Lucas was placed on permanent disability by his physician and began to receive some government assistance. He went for psychiatric treatment and entered into an outreach rehabilitation program for youths with drug and alcohol problems. With treatment, his memory disorder improved, he got off drugs and started going to a gym to strengthen his body. He also took medications for his depression and OCD and began to gradually improve.

Finally, after a few years of treatment, he settled his claim through mediation. He used this money to upgrade his high school education, took a public-speaking course, moved his mother out of the dilapidated basement suite and into a low-cost rental condo and looked after her.

After another two years, he became a volunteer working with local addictions programs and started up information groups for young people his age. He went from school to school with videos of himself and his injuries and talked about his experiences dealing with depression, OCD and addictions.

The local police and prison departments hired him to speak to addicted prisoners, which is where I first heard his story. He walked with a cane and his leg was in a steel brace, but he said he had a new outlook on life and enjoyed travelling around his community speaking to groups, and even making some money!

CHAPTER 18

Neurologists, Neurosurgeons and Neuropsychologists

Dr. Sun Cho Li

The traffic was light as Dr. Sun Cho Li drove to the downtown eye clinic. This morning he would be demonstrating his famous surgical procedure on extracting a fibrous retinal membrane from the back of the eyeball to a large group of medical students. He turned into the parking garage and flicked his monthly pass at the digital remote. The steel gate silently lifted and he drove through, stopping his car on the opposite side, wanting to speak to the attendant in the ticket booth about a problem with his reserved parking spot.

He got out of the SUV, waved to the attendant and stepped towards the booth. That was precisely when the steel gate came down directly on the top of Dr. Li's head.

Stunned and dazed, he stumbled into the opposite lane and was hit by a vehicle coming down the ramp. Dr. Li was knocked down, striking his head against the curb.

The man from the ticket booth ran to his side, screaming for help as he mopped away blood from a gash on Dr. Li's forehead. The driver who hit him called 911.

An ambulance arrived and took the doctor to the emergency department of the hospital, which was less than half a block away. An ER physician examined Dr. Li and ordered X-rays, a CT scan and an MRI.

"I'll call in a neurologist," the ER physician said, as he read the admission reports. "You've had a concussion, Dr. Li. You're confused, your speech is slurred, your right hand is weak and I'm told you stumble when you walk."

Li made slow progress, and after six months he was placed on long-term disability. His doctor was worried about Dr. Li's continuing memory problem and ongoing inability to walk without staggering. A second CT scan showed possible bleeding in his brain.

A month later Dr. and Mrs. Li met with their family physician.

"Dr. Li, I'm going to refer you to a neurologist for more specialized tests and to a neuropsychologist to get an evaluation on your memory disorder."

Dr. Li's wife looked grim. This had been a tough time for her too.

"I'll also set up an appointment for you to see a neuro-surgeon," the doctor said, "because of that second CT scan. It shows there might still be some bleeding in the skull."

Neurologists, neurosurgeons and neuropsychologists

Three different specialists with the same name tag, '*neuro*' in front of their specialty! Are you confused yet? Many people are, but if you have had a head injury or a body injury affecting your nervous system, you could be referred to one or even all three of these consultants. Briefly, the neurologist and the neurosurgeon are both medical doctors while the neuropsychologist is a highly-trained individual who specializes in testing and treating memory, or cognitive, disorders.

After you've seen any of these specialists, they may write a report to your lawyer or to your doctor, depending on who referred you to them. They might also continue to treat you, together with your family physician, or make further suggestions for more evaluations and longer-term therapy.

Neurologists

Neurologists are medical doctors who specialize in the diagnosis and treatment of nervous system disorders, which affect the brain, spinal cord, nerves or muscles. Some specialize even further, that is, they may choose to focus on a certain area of neurological conditions such as stroke or blood vessel problems, seizure disorders (convulsions and epilepsy) or neuromuscular illnesses like multiple sclerosis and amyotrophic lateral sclerosis or ALS (also known as Lou Gehrig's Disease).

When you are referred to a neurologist, she might take a personal and family history and give you a thorough examination to test and evaluate your nervous system. Tests might focus on your muscles, balance, walking ability, reflexes, sensations, memory or speech. She might also order additional tests like blood work, scans, MRIs or more complicated tests through a special lab or clinic. The neurologist may then review all the test results to determine what type of injury your brain may have sustained or what other parts of your nervous system could be affected by your accident. These results can then be presented in a medical-legal letter to your lawyer or to the insurance company. This document answers questions that referring doctors might have asked to have addressed and provides a diagnosis or suggestions as to what treatments might be needed.

Dr. Li

It was clear that Dr. Li had memory problems, difficulty speaking clearly, weakness in his hand, trembling and staggering when walking. The neurologist reviewed all the tests that had been ordered to determine what type of injury his brain sustained and what other parts of the nervous system might have been affected by the accident. With this information, the neurologist wrote a medical-legal letter to Dr. Li's lawyer and to the insurance company, with a diagnosis and what treatments might be needed.

Neurosurgeons

Neurosurgeons are medical doctors who specialize in the diagnosis and surgical treatments of neurological disorders or traumas to the brain. They also deal with spinal problems like narrowing of the spinal cord or tumors. Neurosurgeons are trained to surgically repair nerve tumors or injuries to the nerves anywhere in the body or relieve pressure in the brain, if there is bleeding.

Neurosurgeons may act just like neurologists in examining patients thoroughly. Patients may be frustrated when they are asked to go over and over the same material, but it is very important that the specialist has all this information. The examination and recommendation for any further tests may then be documented in a report to a family doctor, lawyer or insurance company.

Dr. Li

Dr. Li's CAT scan and MRI revealed a subdural hematoma, (bleeding) under the heavy sheath that protects the brain from the inside of the skull. After reviewing the case, the neurosurgeon recommended surgery, explaining that he would make a small hole in Dr. Li's skull, which would permit him to vacuum out the blood clot and relieve the pressure. While this is a serious situation, it is a very common procedure, and Dr. Li decided to go ahead with the surgery.

After months of rehabilitation he was able to get out of his wheelchair and start moving around independently. As his walking improved, his muscles got stronger and his tremors stopped. However, his memory was still poor and, for that reason, he was referred to a neuropsychologist.

Neuropsychologists

Neuropsychologists first receive a degree in psychology, then a postgraduate degree that focuses on the psychological aspects of neurological disorders. Often they will have a PhD after their names and, therefore, will be called doctor. However, they are not medical doctors, so patients may have to pay privately for their services. Neuropsychologists are fully registered by their own professional college in the jurisdiction in which they practice. They usually focus their practices on assessing cognitive disorders, or difficulties with thought, concentration and memory.

Before meeting a neuropsychologist, a lawyer or doctor may send him or her reports of your progress since the accident and request answers to questions about your memory. After reviewing the reports, the neuropsychologist may meet with you and ask how the injury has affected your memory, ability to concentrate and lifestyle. This might include questions as to what extent life at home and relationships with friends, family or work associates has been complicated by forgetfulness, an inability to multitask, confusion, distractibility, fatigue or disinterest.

After a prolonged interview, the neuropsychologist might give you a long series of tests. These may be designed to measure personality or an intelligence test to determine your Intelligence Quotient (IQ) to see if there has been any deterioration in your intelligence following the accident. Other tests may determine what emotional or psychological complications you might have such as depression, anxiety, panic or post-traumatic stress, while still others test language problems, problem-solving, planning, organizational skills and orientation as to place, person and time. This process can be exhausting, which is why the examination may take several hours or even a couple of days to complete.

Upon completion of all the tests and interviews, the neuro-psychologist may provide an extensive report on the results. This can include a conclusion and a diagnosis and might also make suggestions as to treatment. This report may then be sent to the doctor or lawyer who ordered it.

Dr. Li

The neuropsychologist spent several hours assessing Dr. Li. The diagnosis was a moderate to severe traumatic brain injury caused by the blow to his head when he struck the curb. The neuropsychologist wrote that the prognosis could be favourable with time, which could allow the brain to heal, and also recommended therapy. Dr. Li was referred to an occupational therapist and to a rehabilitation treatment centre to learn techniques to improve both his memory and his communication skills. Dr. Li also met with a language speech therapist to improve his ability to articulate (that is, to speak clearly).

Dr. Li followed through with all of the recommendations. After another two years of therapy, he was very much improved in all his functions. Unfortunately, he had lost his ability to do the fine, exacting and precise eye surgery he spent so many years learning. However, he found work with other ophthalmologists, and continues to examine people for eye disorders. He is still able to prescribe medication and make recommendations for surgery.

He remains hopeful, has an understanding wife and family and helpful friends. He exercises as much as possible at his local gym and follows his physicians' recommendations. After such a serious injury, he is still able to enjoy life and still has satisfying and useful work.

CHAPTER 19

Orthopedic Surgeons, Occupational Therapists and Rehabilitation Specialists

Jaspreet

It was a wretched night in mid-December when Jaspreet's boss called just before midnight.

"Jaz, there's a burst water main at Trunk Road on Number One. A cave-in!" his boss shouted into the phone. "I've got the crew ready with the heavy equipment. Got to clear it before the morning rush!"

Jaspreet dressed in his reflective yellow suit and heavy boots and arrived at the chaotic scene within the hour. Marilyn, his co-worker, was already diverting traffic around the gaping hole in the highway as a backhoe ran back and forth filling it. It had finally stopped snowing, but traffic was backed up for a good mile. Marilyn was letting the cars through one by one.

Jaz waved to her as he placed several bright red cones and 'Slow Down' and 'Road Repair' signs on his side of the highway. By 2 a.m. the traffic had thinned and he and Marilyn had everything under control, alternating the flow of traffic.

He heard the steady honking of an impatient driver three cars back on his side of the road. He had turned his sign to 'Stop', since Marilyn was moving cars on her side. Jaz waved his sign up high, so that the honker could see it, and turned to get out of the way as the backhoe swung in his direction.

At that moment, the impatient driver pulled onto the shoulder of the road and sped past the two cars in front of him. He ran directly into Jaz, who was hurled through the air and was slammed into the steel bucket of the backhoe. The driver sped away, never stopping.

Jaz slid down in a heap as workers and the other two drivers rushed to his aid. They knew not to move him. They called 911, and covered him in their coats. The ambulance took him to the nearest hospital where X-rays showed he had four fractured vertebrae in his back, a fractured right femur, a dislocated right shoulder and a concussion.

For several months after the surgeries to his spine and leg, Jaz still couldn't remember the accident, the car honking, or even his own phone number or address. Now he was in a wheelchair, permanently disabled as a paraplegic with paralysis from the waist down. He was on long-term disability and would never return to his job with the city.

Jaz's lawyer referred him to an orthopedic surgeon for a medical-legal opinion and to a psychiatrist for an opinion and for therapy. The lawyer also recommended an occupational therapist, who would evaluate his needs to get around his home, garden and community. Jaz also had an appointment with a rehabilitation therapist to see what therapies he needed to help him function at his best.

Orthopedic surgeons, occupational therapists and rehabilitation specialists

Very soon after a motor vehicle accident, or MVA, your physician or your lawyer may refer you to an orthopedic surgeon to evaluate the physical injuries to your bones, joints, tendons and muscles. He might then refer you to an occupational therapist or a rehabilitation consultant to assess your physical abilities and determine what devices, mechanical or otherwise, you may be able to use to make life easier for you. The rehabilitation therapist can also assess what future therapies and remedies will help allow you to function at your best in spite of ongoing, long-lasting disabilities.

Orthopedic surgeons

Orthopedic surgeons are medical doctors who specialize in conditions dealing with the muscles, tendons and the skeleton. An orthopedic surgeon will likely want to speak with you to understand what injuries you have suffered. Then she will do a physical examination. This can be uncomfortable, as the doctor will have to move, pull or twist those parts of your body that are injured and painful in order to fully understand your injury. These examinations may enable the orthopedic surgeon to provide a medical-legal report or an independent medical evaluation report to your lawyer or the referring doctor. However, if examining you for an IME, the surgeon *may not* give you any information about that examination as to diagnosis or treatments. Legal rules state that IMEs must be independent and not for therapeutic purposes.

The examination will be very thorough in order for the surgeon to provide a medical opinion and diagnosis in written reports. These reports may also provide a prognosis, whereby the doctor uses her medical expertise to determine what the future state of your injuries might be, what treatment options are available to get you healthy again and how long these treatments could take. If you are seen quite soon after the motor vehicle accident, it may not be possible for the surgeon to arrive at a *final* opinion or prognosis, as you will likely require further evaluation after any surgeries or therapies are completed. Her report to your doctor or lawyer might also include recommendations for further referrals to either an occupational therapist or rehabilitation specialist, or both.

Occupational therapists

An occupational therapist, or OT, may spend considerable time with you to provide a report. This report might suggest whether you need any specialized equipment to improve your ability to live and function independently with your new limitations. Some examples are ergonomic chairs, bathtub bars, safety equipment or special devices for your kitchen, home or employment. A consultation with an OT could take several hours or even a few days and could include meetings in your home, your workplace or in the office of the occupational therapist or at all three places.

An OT can assess how you are managing with your disabilities in your home, in your community and in your employment (if you are able to return to work). He might attempt to help you to change your lifestyle so that you can continue to live as comfortably as possible, function at your best and improve your organization and performance in everyday activities. If you are now in a wheelchair, you may also need various types of equipment in your home such as ramps, special tables, chairs, bathtub bars, toilet seats or showers that you can access from your wheelchair.

Your lawyer might also request that the OT produce a detailed report focusing on your home environment, your social and leisure activity, your employment, your general daily living activities, your ability to manage your own care or a combination of some or all of these. The reports might also include a lengthy and detailed 'cost of future care' section, with an assessment of the costs required to enable you to participate fully in your home, your community and your employment, and discuss your reported functioning in these areas prior to the accident. Finally, the OT may provide a professional opinion as to your abilities and limitations. The report may note whether you need community support services or treatments such as massage or physiotherapy. It may also consider medication costs or make recommendations for psychiatric treatment, a pain-disorder clinic or vocational counseling and identify whether or not you are able to return to your same job or require training in a new occupation.

Rehabilitation specialists

The orthopedic surgeon, the occupational therapist or your lawyer may recommend that you see yet another medical doctor, the rehabilitation specialist, also called a *physiatrist*. This individual may examine you and may make further suggestions to help restore you to your former position of good health, or as normal a life as possible with your present and possibly permanent disability. Suggestions made by the rehabilitation specialist might also have been made by the two previous specialists, but this consultation may be more detailed as to the therapy you will require in the future with your longer-lasting disabilities.

If you are referred to a rehabilitation consultant, you will be seeing an individual who is a specialist in physical medicine and rehabilitation, which deals with the diagnosis of ongoing injuries or physical conditions. Physiatrists can assess and help you manage spinal, musculoskeletal and neurological injuries expected to be permanent. If there is no likelihood that you will function as you did prior to the accident, this specialist will make recommendations to help you function with your now-normal permanent disability.

When you meet with a rehabilitation specialist, expect him to also take a history and examine you just as the other specialists did. Again, he will likely want to know how you were functioning before the accident, what happened to you in the accident and the kind of limitations that you experienced following the accident. He can also produce a report as to your ability to function in your daily living activities such as managing your own care and doing household chores. Your ability to work and participate in activities such as sports or volunteer work might also be noted.

These reports may also provide various professional opinions and suggestions, a prognosis or recommendations for further evaluations and treatments. There could be specific recommendations for present and future medication, an exercise program with a specialist in a gymnasium and further psychological or psychiatric treatment. It could also suggest vocational testing and planning with education or retraining for alternate employment. For example, if you are now in a wheelchair, you may still be capable of going to college or university, of learning a new trade or profession or be employable in sedentary positions.

Jaspreet

I heard about Jaz again many years later when his nephew Mandeep was referred to me for depression. I had seen Jaz on a number of occasions back then because he was so pessimistic about life and needed antidepressants.

"So, what happened to your uncle?" I asked the nephew.

Mandeep thought for a few minutes. "Well, he had a bad time there for a while. His family got fed up with him. His wife left him because he was so nasty, always yelling and throwing things."

"Oh, sorry to hear that. Poor fellow," I said, thinking that was the last I'd hear about Jaz, and getting ready to ask Mandeep about his own depression.

Mandeep was a slow talker and even a slower thinker with his depressive disorder, but he raised his eyes at me and said, "Well, not so poor, doctor. In fact he made a fortune as an accountant and bought up a bunch of land in the valley to grow blueberries."

"A fortune in blueberries?" I asked.

"Well, sort of," Mandeep said with a sigh.

Slowly he continued, and I was glad that I was patient. "First he went back to college and got his Bachelor's degree and then got his CGA, you know, an accountant certification."

I was amazed . . . in fact, I was completely flabbergasted. "But he had a head injury. That's why he was so irritable and violent to his family."

"Oh, yeh, yeh. Well, he got over that with some pills that a doctor ordered for him. He sees his wife and kids now. He did well as an accountant sitting in a wheelchair in his office. Liked figures, he did. Very fussy, you know persnickety-like."

"Persnickety? Well, you need to be that way to be a good accountant," I added, smiling.

"Yeah, yeah, that's it," Mandeep said, "He saw some other shrink who told him he was good with figures. So that's what he did. He bought up all that land and grew blueberries. Now I work for him in his blueberry exporting business."

'Amazing,' I thought. 'Just amazing! You just never know.'

CHAPTER 20

Physiotherapy, Massage Therapy, Chiropractic Therapy, Pilates and Pastoral Counseling

Alexandra

It was a good morning so far. The weather had been perfect for Alexandra's five-mile run. She had made good time, and now, showered and fed, she was driving to work in her brand-new Honda. There were only ten more days left in her summer job. Grad school was beginning! Yes, life was good.

A road-construction sign warned drivers to slow down, and a flagwoman was directing traffic. Alexandra pulled up behind the two vehicles stopped in front of her. She had just opened her window to get some fresh air when she heard a loud bang and, as the airbag deployed, her Honda shot forward into the back of the car in front of her.

"Are you all right, miss?" the flagger asked, pushing the airbag away from Alexandra's face.

Alexandra felt a severe pinching sensation in her neck and felt dazed as she got out of her car and looked at her rear bumper. "I . . . I think so, thanks. Just a sore neck and a bit of a headache."

She stared back and forth at the crumpled rear bumper and front grille. "Look at that will you. My brand-new car." But the flagger was already rushing away to check on the occupant of the other car.

Shaken, Alexandra exchanged information with the other driver and got the flagger's name as a witness. She drove her crumpled car straight home and tried to relax for the rest of the day. The following morning she found she couldn't turn her head, her back ached and she couldn't walk for the pain in her back and knee. She saw her physician, who gave her a prescription for Tylenol with codeine and suggested massage therapy. The doctor also gave her a short note for her employer for time off work. But the pain persisted, forcing her to sleep on the floor. Headaches made it difficult for her to fall asleep.

Two weeks later she followed up with her doctor because of continuing body pain. Her doctor wrote to the insurance company saying that Alexandra could no longer run, was having difficulty sleeping and couldn't work or attend school because of whiplash, chronic headaches and soft-tissue injuries to her back and knee. He also gave her a referral to a physiotherapist.

Alexandra's good friend Diana was sympathetic to the problems she was facing and suggested that she talk to a lawyer she knew. Diana made an appointment with the lawyer for the next day.

Alexandra angrily slammed her fist on the lawyer's desk. "Damn! It was such a small accident and now look at me," she said crossly, pointing to her neck brace.

After hearing the story, the lawyer suggested that Alexandra needed further evaluations with an orthopedic surgeon, but warned that it could take some time before an appointment could be arranged. She was told to continue with physiotherapy in the meantime.

Physiotherapy, massage therapy, chiropractic therapy, Pilates and pastoral counseling

Following an accident, your physician or lawyer may refer you to a physiotherapist, massage therapist or a chiropractor. Further rehabilitation may also be available privately through a pastoral counselor or by joining a Pilates or yoga group. Consult your physician if you are unsure of your progress in therapy, as you might need further assessments or referrals to other consultants.

Physiotherapists

Physiotherapists work with you to help you return to the best physical strength possible following your MVA injuries. Physiotherapists are university-trained and registered with the provincial College of Physical Therapists. Ask the physiotherapist about his qualifications and expertise.

During your first appointment, your physiotherapist will generally take a medical history in order to develop a program for you. This might include specific questions about the accident and your complaints, or *symptoms*. He will likely examine you, focusing on the specific area of your pain and disability to determine current benchmarks on which to build your therapy. Some focus on the musculoskeletal (muscles and bones) systems, while others are specific towards soft-tissue injuries such as those caused by whiplash.

Physiotherapists are usually trained in diagnosing and treating fractures, sprains, strains, joint problems and back and neck pain. Treatment can include a number of different therapies including mobilization, manipulation, traction, therapeutic exercise, hot or cold packs, electrical muscle stimulation or ultrasound mechanical wave stimulation. Make sure to ask your physiotherapist what treatments he plans to use, the goals of each sort of treatment and if there are any extra costs involved.

She will most likely encourage further therapy or might suggest you continue with further investigations and consultations with an occupational or rehabilitation therapist. But you should consult with your physician or lawyer before taking any action. This could include the development of a long-term exercise program with a trainer at a local gym or recommendations for work modification procedures such as different sitting or standing positions in your job. Physiotherapists occasionally make recommendations for the purchase of special equipment like chairs or braces to reduce your pain at home or at work. She may also recommend a psychological assessment and treatment if you seem anxious or depressed or, if you have persistent pain, that you talk with your physician or lawyer for a referral to a chronic pain disorder clinic. Remember to consult your physician if you are in any way unsure of the treatment or your progress.

Alexandra

Alexandra's treatment with her physiotherapist was very extensive. Initially her therapist worked hard to reduce her neck, back and knee pain. The prognosis improved and in the next several weeks the focus moved to increasing muscular function and pain-free movements to try to return Alexandra to normal activities around the house.

With increased stretching, using ice at home and exercise therapy, Alexandra made slow but constant improvement.

Massage therapists

Massage therapists have studied at a qualified massage therapy college. They work to help restore physical function and to relieve pain through active muscular massage, joint mobilization, hydrotherapy or rehabilitative exercises, which may include stretching, strengthening and postural exercises. They provide verbal and written education programs on how to deal with pain and disability. Ask the masseuse about her qualifications and expertise. Your lawyer may cover some of the fees, or payment may be private, but talk with your lawyer first about this possibility. Some extended medical plans also cover some or all of the costs of massage.

Patients see massage therapists to assist with conditions like migraine, tension headaches, tendonitis, arthritic conditions, fibromyalgia and other muscular injuries after an injury. Manipulation, that is, moving and handling your muscles and joints, can be helpful and therapeutic. Massage therapists do bodywork, manual therapy, breathing exercises, dance or movement therapies. They work the connective ligaments and tendons, if these have been bruised or overly stretched in an accident. Massaging the different layers of muscle can help to restore their function and encourage improvement. Talk to your physician if you are unsure of the progress of any therapy. You may require further medical assessment or referrals to other types of consultants.

Alexandra

When Alexandra saw Francine, a young but very experienced massage therapist, she asked her for more information about what type of therapy she would receive.

"We know that manipulation, that is, moving and handling your muscles and joints, is helpful and therapeutic," *Francine explained. "The connective ligaments and tendons might have been aggravated through bruising or being overly stretched. Massaging the different layers of muscles may help to restore their function."*

"So what exactly will you do?" Alexandra asked.

Francine continued, "I'll slowly and carefully manipulate your neck, back and all other relevant muscles with gentle pressure. I may also use vibration tools or other mechanical aids."

Alexandra agreed to be treated by the massage therapist. She lay down on the therapy bed, which was warmed by an electric blanket, relaxed and let the therapist do her work.

Francine talked as she worked on Alexandra's muscles. "I can feel your muscles are very tense. This type of therapy may help relax you and help with your pain, anxiety and depression. It might even help you to sleep better."

Alexandra was pleased to hear that. She had been quite anxious about her grad program studies, with very little sleep and a sore neck and knee.

As Francine slowly massaged Alexandra's back and gently manipulated her neck for greater range of movement, Alexandra felt the tension drain away. She left the therapist's office without her neck brace, already looking forward to her next appointment.

Chiropractors

Chiropractors belong to a professional organization, the provincial College of Chiropractors, which regulates the profession and requires full registration. After four years of study and an internship through an accredited school, a student receives a Doctor of Chiropractic degree. You may be referred to a chiropractor or see one on your own, but be sure to check whether your insurance plan assists you with the fees. Some employers offer extended medical plans that may pay for chiropractic consultations and treatment. If a lawyer refers you to a chiropractor, he may pay for the services out of any settlement agreement.

Chiropractors use physical manipulation and adjustments of the joints or spine to help patients acquire a normal range of motion. The chiropractor may take a medical history before examining your spine or joints for bone changes and partial dislocations. X-rays could also be required for some injuries. Chiropractors can treat whiplash injuries with stretching, massage, adjustments and physical therapy methods.

Your prognosis may be much better if you seek early evaluation and treatment with any of the above therapists, but some therapists suggest that you wait a few days, until after the swelling and inflammation has gone down. See your family doctor for an opinion if you are uncertain about when you should see any of these therapists.

Pilates

Pilates instructors are trained to provide body and mind wellness, treating the mind and body as one, using resistance techniques. Modern-day Pilates may use mats and various apparatuses and equipment to train the body. Group interaction may encourage an optimistic outlook to those recovering from injuries. Once again, ask the instructor for his or her qualifications and expertise. Speak to your family doctor before embarking on this type of program.

Pastoral Counseling

Religious counseling is included here as it can help individuals struggling with some form of psychological or physical pain. A spiritual mentor may help restore your general health and well-being. Generally, physicians or lawyers do not refer or suggest such counseling and do not request reports from them.

Many rabbis, priests and ministers have special training in spiritual counseling and use spiritual and psychological understandings to help in healing. Many are also trained in psychology, philosophy, ethics, biblical history, world religions and the psychology of religion. Having a deep religious faith may improve your psychological health. Religious counselors may be helpful to sufferers in a dilemma about the meaning of life, or who have critical health issues and are seeking answers to questions that other professionals shy away from. Some religious counselors have a close association with other community services and mental health workers.

Some victims of life-altering accidents have felt that life or the future is no longer an option for them and claim that their faith renewed their optimism and gave them the strength to continue.

If you wish such counseling, take the initiative, find it on your own.

Alexandra

Alexandra followed through with physiotherapy, and was also treated by a massage therapist. She gradually improved and, after a few months, was able to start jogging again. Three years after the accident, she entered a half-marathon.

She completed her graduate studies and a social work program. Her credentials are impressive: "BSW, MSW, Social Worker, Community Mental Health Services."

Two years after the accident, on her lawyer's advice and a short discovery session with the insurance company lawyer, Alexandra agreed to a settlement.

CHAPTER 21

Safe Walking, Cycling and Driving

Kamiko

A crowd of office workers was waiting for the traffic light to change. The pedestrian sign still warned 'Stop' and a green arrow began flashing for drivers turning left. Just then, Kamiko's phone buzzed. Takumi, her husband, was calling from Nagasaki, possibly about his employment interview with Mitsubishi. Kamiko pulled her hoodie up so she could focus on the conversation with Takumi and clicked the answer icon. The job was his! Kamiko was so excited that she forgot all about her surroundings. She stepped off the curb, into the crosswalk and into a bus that was turning left.

Kamiko was lucky that day. She hit the bus with her head down but with her right hand up, holding the phone, which shielded her face, and turned quickly. The bus hit her only a glancing blow, so that her shoulder glanced off the bus. She was startled and dropped her phone, but didn't fall down or feel any pain. The bus driver didn't even feel the small thump against his vehicle and continued driving. A man ran out to steady her, picked up her mobile and asked if she was alright.

Kamiko was so embarrassed, she just nodded. She uttered shy thanks, took the phone and ran back to the curb.

"Hello? Hello? Oh, there you are," her husband asked over the phone. "What happened? I lost you for a minute, Kamiko."

"Oh, nothing, nothing," Kamiko said. "It was nothing, Takumi. I was lucky, just a slight fall. It was nothing." Her heart raced and her stomach heaved.

It was indeed her lucky day. Three seconds earlier and she could have been seriously injured. She could have been killed. Takumi could have lost his wife forever . . .

Safe walking, cycling and driving

There are many books, pamphlets and articles about walking, cycling and driving safely, which I advise you to read. Be a good example, talk to your friends and family about safety. Books, etc., are available at community centres, bookstores, libraries and sports stores. You may also find information at police and fire departments. You could take one of the numerous defensive driving instructional programs, researching what is available in your community.

Walking

Think about the following simple rules when you are taking a walk. Be aware of your surroundings at all times and in all venues, particularly on trails that are accessible to ATVs, motorbikes or mountain bikes. Be responsible for your own safety. Pedestrian are vulnerable — don't take it for granted that drivers and cyclists see you or that they will be able to stop or avoid you.

Drivers of cars, bicycles and motorcycles are supposed to stop for you at crosswalks, but don't count on it. The driver may be distracted: talking to passengers, on a phone, texting, changing the air conditioner settings or radio station. Be careful, pay attention, look around you as you cross streets. Take a flashlight, wear light colours or reflective clothing at night and when it is raining — dark colours are hard for drivers to see. Bright colours stand out more clearly against the snow. And remember, whoever has the right of way doesn't matter — you are no match for a 2,000-pound vehicle.

On a roadway without a sidewalk, walk on the left side, facing the traffic. Look right and left at a controlled intersection to make sure a car or cyclist is not turning into your path. Make eye contact with drivers of all types of vehicles and wave to make sure that he or she stops while you are in the crosswalk.

Don't cover your ears in winter, and don't impair your vision with a hoodie. Listening to music and talking on your cell phone while walking interferes with your ability to be aware of your surroundings. Keep your dog on a short leash to prevent it from running out into traffic and causing an accident.

Cycling

Always wear a helmet when cycling. Use hand signals when changing lanes and use both reflective clothing and lights at night. Obey the rules of the road and ride as if other drivers can't see you. If you are not aware of the rules of the road, you may find a pamphlet at bike stores, your local police or fire department, library or community centre. Weaving in and out of traffic, changing lanes without signaling and making turns to the left or right into oncoming traffic may cause an accident. Use designated bicycle lanes or routes, if available.

An all-too-common accident for cyclists is collision with a car door. Drivers don't always check their rear-view mirrors or blind spots as they open the door. The driver is likely at fault, but that won't help as you go slam into the door.

Driving

Drive defensively! Keep your eyes moving, so that you are aware of what is going on all around you. Make sure the rear-view mirror and side-view mirrors provide a clear and unobstructed view, shoulder-check when changing lanes and avoid following the vehicle in front of you too closely — have time to react if something happens ahead of you. That is, *do not tailgate!*

Make sure your car is in good working order, that lights, horn, windshield wipers and brakes are all working correctly. Use turn signals when changing lanes and maintain a safe, consistent speed on the freeway. Be especially careful when you are using the ramps on or off a freeway. *Never* stop on the freeway unless it is an emergency. Be especially careful as you pass an accident scene and stay clear of emergency vehicles. Seniors who drive should be extra vigilant — as we become older, our reaction time may not be as quick.

This is just a short summary of what you can do to protect yourself while driving, cycling or walking.

Be smart. Walk, cycle and drive smart.

CHAPTER 22

Prognosis

Throughout this book, you have seen the word *prognosis* several times. Prognosis means predicting or telling you something about your illness or disability. It's a word that is used to convey information to other physicians about the possible results of treatments and expected recovery.

Physicians and other health workers use their knowledge and experience to *predict* what may happen to you following an injury, both before and after treatment. A physician or a consultant may make a statement about your prognosis after the first or subsequent consultation. A prognosis may change over time, or with treatment. Occasionally consultants will withhold making a prognosis because he or she believes more investigation is needed.

Here are some of the most common types of prognoses given by physicians:

Excellent

Generally this means that you are expected to recover totally with or even without treatment, to return to your pre-accident level of functioning in a relatively short period of time. This might be because your accident was relatively minor and that you are young, healthy and in good shape.

Good

This implies that you will probably make a full recovery from your injuries, but that recovery might be inhibited by pre-existing conditions. These might be a physical ailment such as diabetes or you may be older and take longer to heal. It might also suggest that you may need more prolonged treatments from several therapists, but that there is a strong likelihood that you will return to a healthy way of functioning.

Fair

This suggests that improvement and full recovery will take longer, possibly because of the severity of your injury, your age, pre-existing illnesses and other possible factors. You could require further treatment from a number of therapists for both your injuries and pre-existing conditions. Fair may also indicate that you need to visit therapists such as rehabilitation consultants.

Poor

This suggests that full recovery may be difficult or take a long time, even with further treatment. Improvements are possible, but you may have to see many therapists and treatment may be prolonged. Even with therapy, recurrences or problems with depression or severe anxiety are expected.

Guarded

A guarded prognosis suggests that recovery is expected to take a very long time and that your condition is fragile. You may require further investigations or evaluations by other specialists and help from community agencies. It may be that a pre-existing illness, previous serious injuries or aged-based complications, compounded by a lack of family or other support, may impede your recovery.

Your prognosis depends on a number of factors:
- the extent and severity of your injury
- past illnesses and any ongoing recurrent illnesses

- past treatments for injuries or illnesses
- family history
- ability to accept and follow through with treatment recommendations
- other stressors in your life or drug or alcohol addictions

These factors help to determine your prognosis. People with a positive, optimistic personality and a close, supportive group of friends or family are more likely to have a favourable future outcome. Those who are happy with their lifestyle, exercise regularly, are involved in voluntary community activities, have a strong faith, avoid addictions and have a balanced way of life tend to see more improvements. These circumstances may change a prognosis. Your physicians may even encourage you to be optimistic.

I hope you have enjoyed and benefited from reading this book. If it helped anyone just a little bit, then writing this book for me was very worthwhile. I wish you all the best in your journey as you travel through the process of dealing with your motor vehicle accident.

Index

paramedics, 60–62
pastoral counseling, 124–25, 129
personal injury claim, 14–15
physicians, family, 64–65, 89–90
physiotherapists, 124–26
Pilates, 124–25, 129
police, legal obligations to, 2, 4–6
post-concussion syndrome (PCS), 81–84
post-traumatic stress disorder (PTSD), 87–90
psychiatrists, 29–31
psychologists, 29–30

Q
Quebec, 7, 9, 11

R
record keeping, 5–6, 12, 65
rehabilitation therapists/therapy, 72, 119–20
religious counseling, 124–25, 129

S
Saskatchewan, 7, 9, 11
sexual/intimate relationships, 21, 34, 102
social anxiety/phobia, 89, 92, 95, 96–97
suing for damages, 10–11

T
therapists/therapy, 97, 116–17, 124–25
chiropractors, 128
massage, 126–27
occupational, 72, 118
physiotherapists, 125–26
Pilates, 129
rehabilitation, 72, 119–20
traumatic brain injury (TBI), 81–83

U
underinsured motorist protection (UMP), 3, 12, 16
United States (USA), 3–4, 51

W
walking, safe, 132–33
whiplash injuries, 76–78
witnesses, character, 51
witnesses, to the accident, 15, 16, 25
Worker's Compensation Act, 7

Acknowledgements

In writing this book, I have been helped enormously by many professionals, both legal and medical, and friends and family. I am very grateful to my wife, Jean, for her patience, support, love and guidance throughout this lengthy process. In addition I wish to thank Marilyn McPhillips and my son, Michael, for their advice and assistance, and my daughter, Diana, who always encouraged me to visualize. I want to express my deep gratitude to my many friends and colleagues who were always encouraging and interested and especially to my editor, Kit Schindell, whose keen perspective and expert direction guided me throughout the completion of this book.

I am indebted to Zack Vilvang, lawyer who gave me his expert guidance in the legal chapters and to Rose A. Keith, trial lawyer who assisted me so kindly with the insurance chapter. I am grateful to my colleague, Dr. James Warren, for his opinions as to the medical sections, and to my United Church minister, Rev. Dr. Ross Lockhart, for his input on the pastoral therapy sections. Finally, I am indebted to Jo Blackmore at Granville Island Publishing and her professional team for their superlative work in helping me to publish this work.

Dr. Lawrence E. Matrick grew up in Winnipeg and later received his degree in Medicine from the Manitoba Medical College. After moving to Vancouver with his wife, he worked at the Provincial Mental Hospital at Riverview for one year as a resident in psychiatry. He continued his studies in psychiatry in London, England and received his British degree in Psychiatry, and later his Fellowship in the Royal College of Physicians and Surgeons of Canada.

As an Assistant Professor in Medicine and Psychiatry at the University of British Columbia, he taught medical students and supervised psychiatric residents at the Vancouver General Hospital while running a full-time private practice in Vancouver for almost 50 years, frequently called to court to testify as an expert witness.

For more information, and to keep abreast of developments in this topic and Dr. Matrick's activities, please visit:

www.lawrencematrick.com